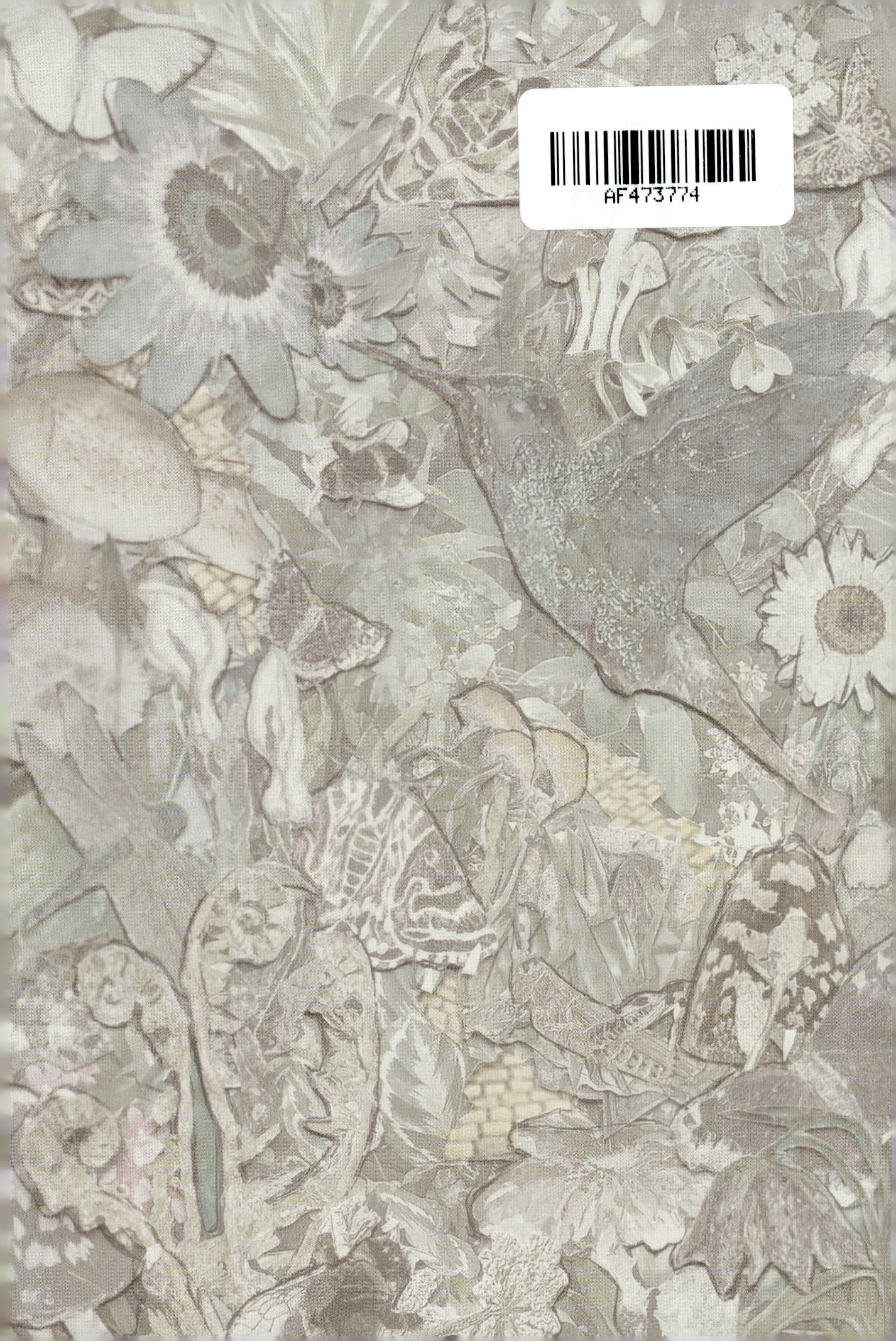

SEASONS FOR THE SOUL

SEASONS FOR THE SOUL

SPELLS OF NATURE

The Embroidered Art of

JULIA VAN DEN BOSCH

UNICORN

For Melia and the Ancestors

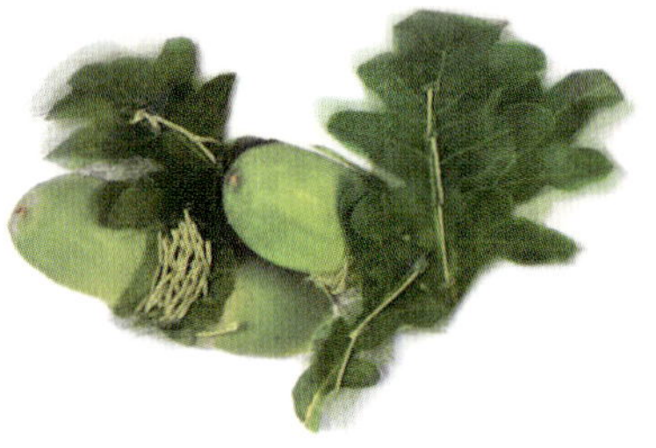

CONTENTS

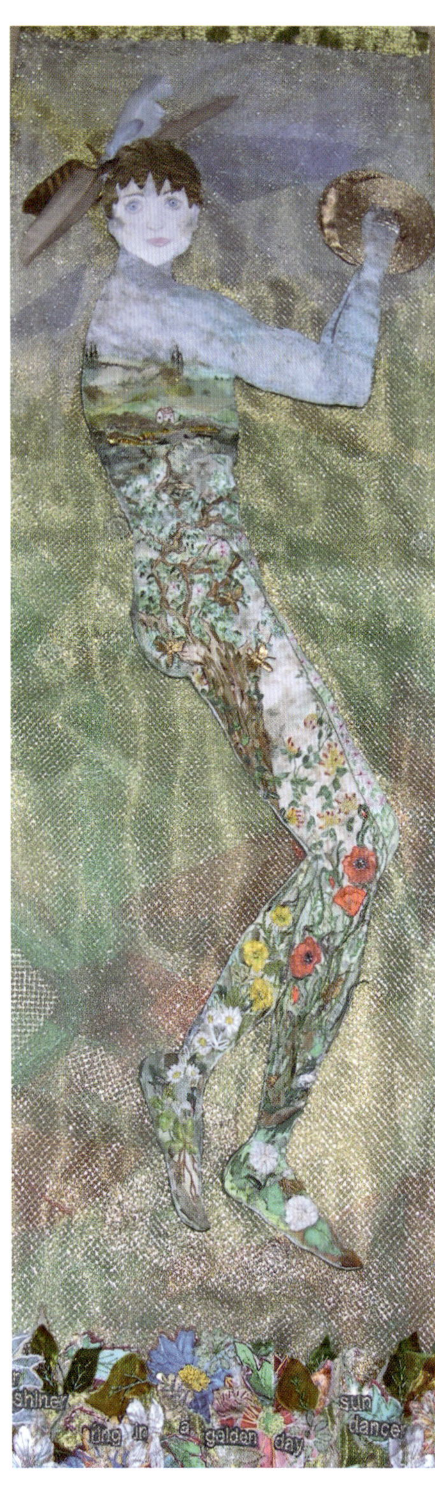
a
golden
day
sun
dancer

INTRODUCTION

I was lucky enough to be raised by storytellers –

spinners of tales in the Celtic tradition. Tales of nature and folklore and wizardry, told to me, in true fairytale fashion, by the fireside or in the deep of the woods or the sunlight of the meadows. Sometimes my grandfather would illustrate the stories as he told them, drawing on the things that surrounded us, so that the magic always stayed present in my imagination wherever I was. It was impossible not to develop a lasting love of nature with such an upbringing, living as we did in the heart of the countryside.

When the pandemic hit many years later, this upbringing was my salvation. Having to shield on my own and seeing no one, nature became not just my lifeline but also my companion, bringing me comfort, solace and friendship. My garden is not a big garden and it is not now in the depths of the countryside but even being enclosed in a small space provided so much life – both expected and unexpected – that there were new discoveries to be made every day and new things to learn and marvel at, with the time to sit and watch and listen.

There is a W.B. Yeats poem that speaks of 'the heaven's embroidered cloths enwrought with golden and silver light', which has always inspired me. This journal is designed to follow the heaven's embroidered cloths and to be an embroidered path to lead through all the natural magic of the seasons, and to bring this path to you wherever you are. In wanting to carry on tradition, my wish is to spin tales through the medium of hand embroidery, using the language of textiles, spinning with threads rather than words. I will see a flower, a plant, a bird or moth or a beautiful bumble bee that captures my imagination. I then want to make that image come alive and try to create its dynamic and its heart for whoever wishes to see it, so that they can discover its world for themselves. To let it tell and share its story as it did to me during the long days of the pandemic. In my small garden, I rediscovered what William Blake meant when he said it was possible 'to see a World in a Grain of Sand And a Heaven in a Wild Flower' and the very action of embroidering these images was in itself a healing joy.

The pandemic led to many people wanting to rediscover nature. It made them more aware of the healing power of nature to the psyche, as an aid to depression, dementia and other mental problems, as well as being an aid to general well-being, even if being in nature was simply working with herbs and flowers in a window box. My small space proved that to be true for me. So having experienced the wonder of this for myself, it has also become a very real aspiration to try to transmit that healing dynamic and energy in my textile work. Hand embroidery is a magical process in that it lets intuition and intent guide the hand, and it encapsulates the art of mindfulness because it allows as much time as is needed to enter fully into an empathetic understanding of the work. To aid me in transmitting this healing energy, I am inserting minuscule fragments of the appropriate crystals into my work. Crystals are also believed to be a part of the healing world, and their different energies are widely recognised. I have worked with crystals for a long time and have fallen under their spell.

This healing aspect of nature includes not only the gift of beauty but also the qualities inherent in the actual plants and trees themselves. We know that many possess medicinal properties, used for centuries across civilisations, from the Amazon rainforest to ancient Egypt; some are complex and relatively unknown, and some, such as aspirin from the bark of the willow tree, are widely recognised. Being in complete isolation, I had the freedom and time to research and learn more about their histories and properties and to find out more about their stories. Researching these facts took me beyond the image in front of me to wherever my imagination wanted to take me in discovery, and that in itself was an adventure, because it enabled me to leave my garden and travel on the wind.

In this journal of the seasons, the embroidered path naturally led me onwards, but there was always time to look to either side of the path, seeing all the many small things that I would not normally notice, because it was the journey rather than the destination that was the important thing to me, and the smallest things would sometimes bring me the greatest delight. The grasshopper swaying on a blade of grass, or a damselfly darting through the reeds, or just watching a dandelion seed floating idly on its way.

As a child I saw, within a cabinet of curiosities, a little stumpwork casket, rich and glowing in the dim light of the shop. The work had created a magical secret world which seemed alive and which invited me to enter, and I was instantly captivated. I hope the embroidered path in this journal will recreate the same magic that the little box of delights offered to me. It comes with love and with intention. And, wherever this path of the seasons takes you, I wish that its story, though small in scale, still bears true witness to the beauty and richness and healing of the land, and that your imagination will take you there in discovery.

IF SEEDS IN THE BLACK EARTH
CAN TURN INTO SUCH BEAUTIFUL ROSES,
WHAT MIGHT NOT THE HEART OF MAN
BECOME IN ITS LONG JOURNEY
TOWARDS THE STARS?

G.K. Chesterton

The unfolding path of the seasons
seen through the eye of a needle.

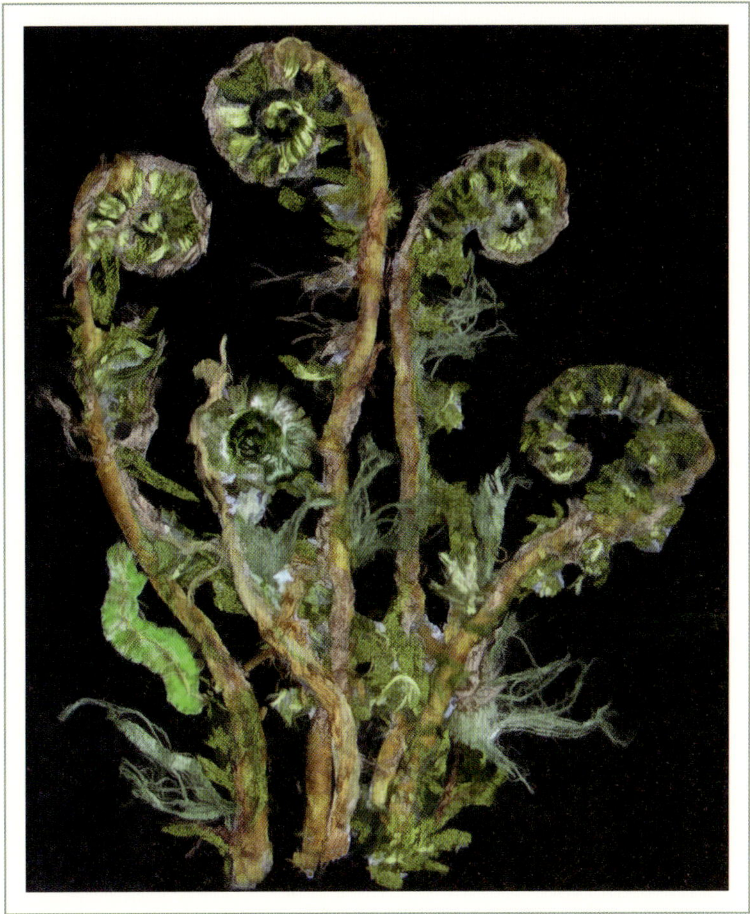

Working in hand embroidery is a magical way to work, and this embroidered path of the seasons uses hand embroidery in its traditional role of storytelling, from spring fritillaria to summer poppy, autumn leaves to seedheads of winter, blackbird to hawk moth. Hand embroidery has been used as a way to record history for centuries, as each stitch the embroiderer makes holds the emotion of the moment, record keeping and journalling. I wanted to use it in this way to record the companionship, healing and nurturing of nature I experienced in isolation. This journal contains just a few of the discoveries I made in the garden from each season, which were also significant markers of the passing of time during that period and which I now, more than ever, appreciate anew each year.

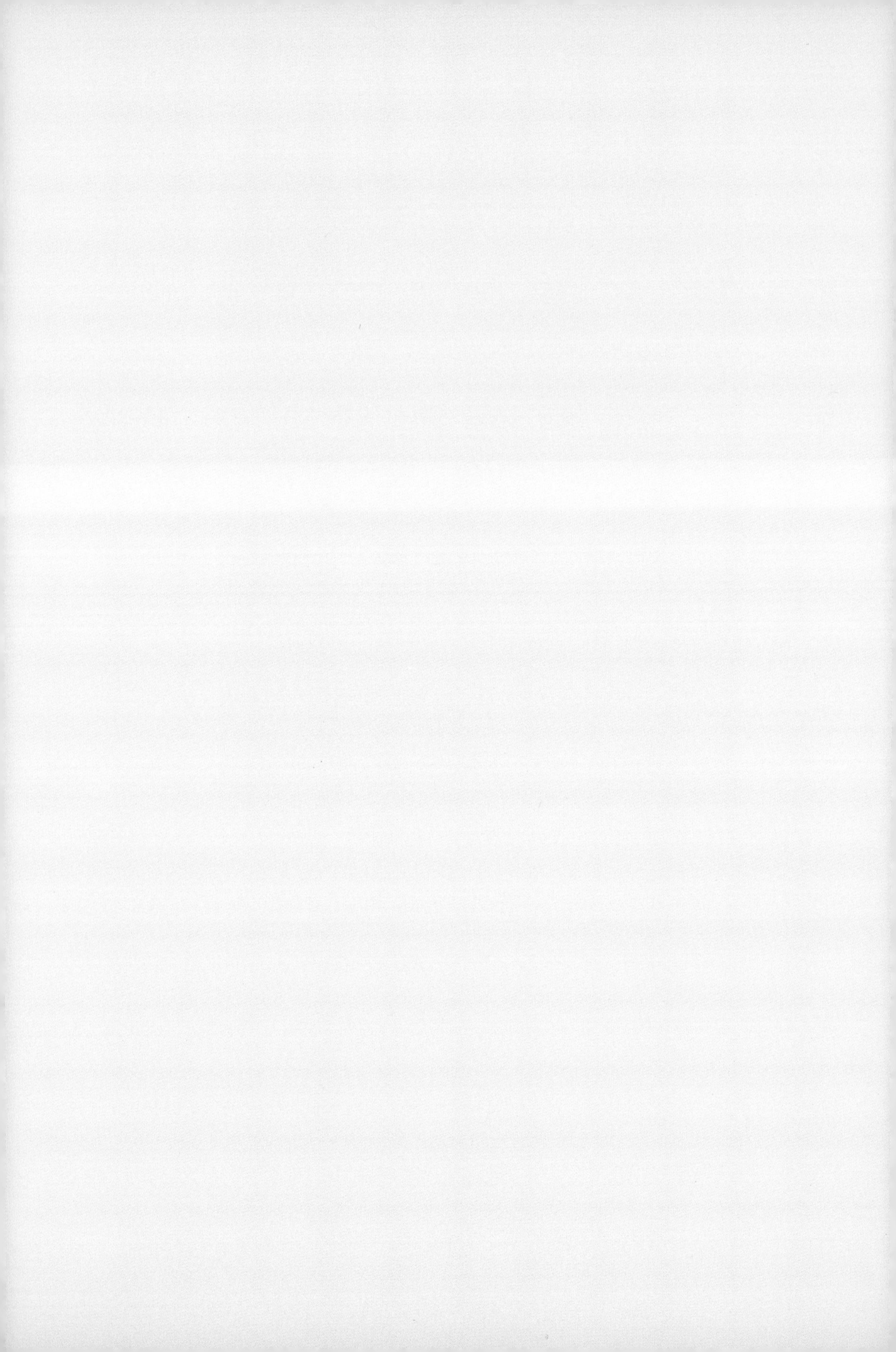

Springtime

After the frozen beauty and stillness of winter, I look forward to the freshness and life of spring, with blackbird singing the first notes of the dawn chorus to waken me every morning.

I have lovely memories of springtime. I think of vivid lime-green leaves. The soft blue mist of the bluebell woods appearing almost overnight and carpets of pure white wood anemones beneath the trees. And the sound of worker bees humming busily in the cherry blossom.

SPRING, this most beautiful of seasons, brings with it the sight of the fritillaria meleagris, one of the early spring flowers. It seems to resemble a lantern of ancient Venetian glass panes, tended by Harlequin, lighting the path for the year to come.

The fritillaria belongs to the lily family but the name for this delicate little flower with its exquisite and intricate colouring is derived from the Latin *fritillus* ('box where dice are kept') due to the distinctive chequered pattern on its petals. It has also collected many other imaginative names to tell its story, such as snake's head, guinea hen flower, chess flower and the very sad name of leper lily – its shape resembles the bell once carried by lepers.

A lovely and evocative flower to embroider with those names in mind, with particles of amethyst, whose properties combine both gentleness and strength, embedded into the work with positive thoughts for the year to come.

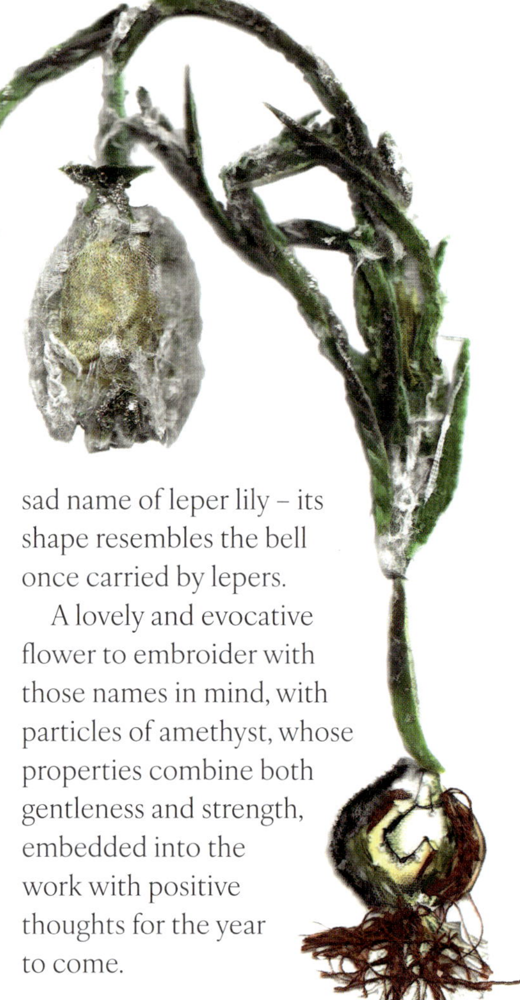

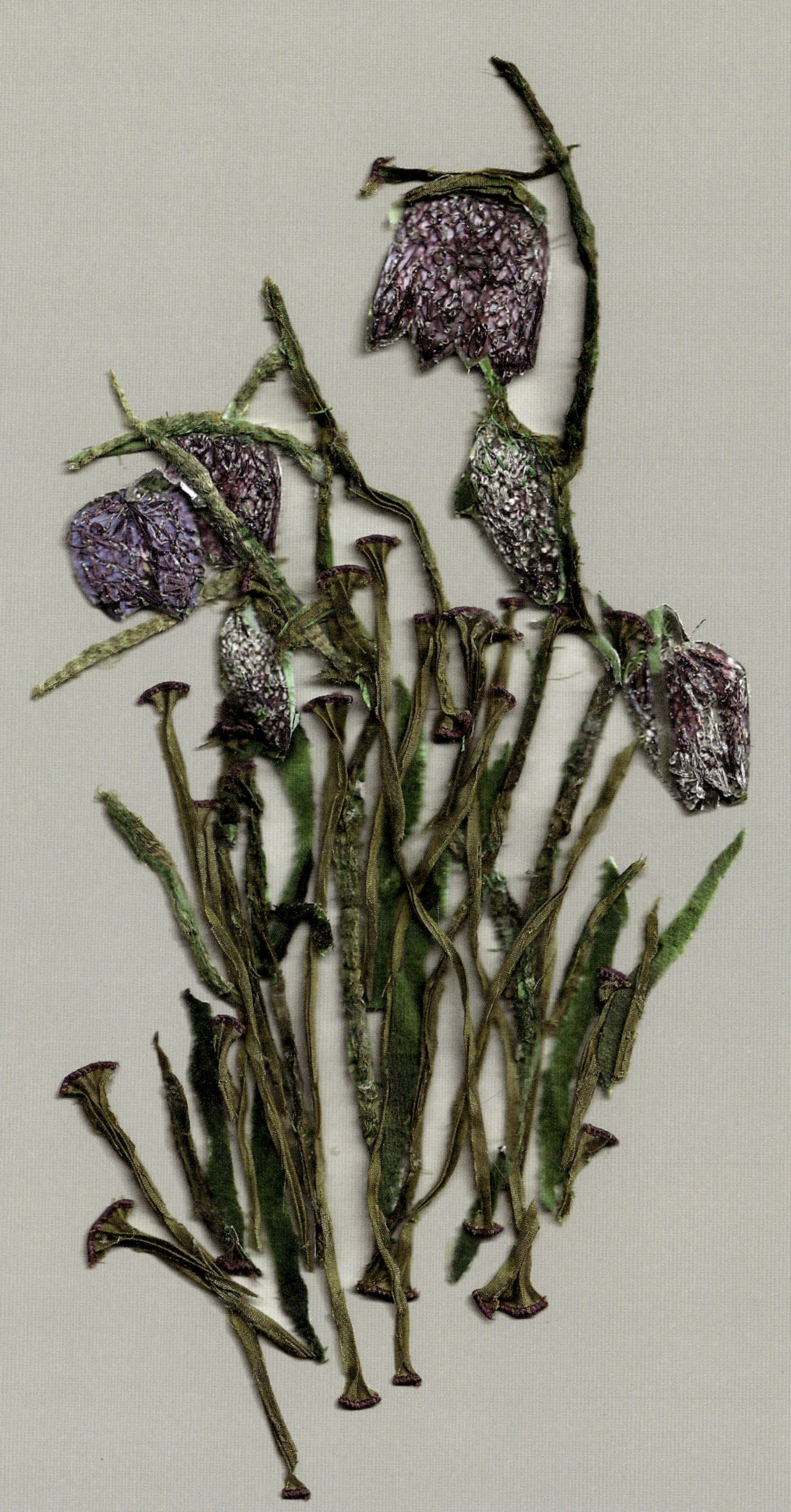

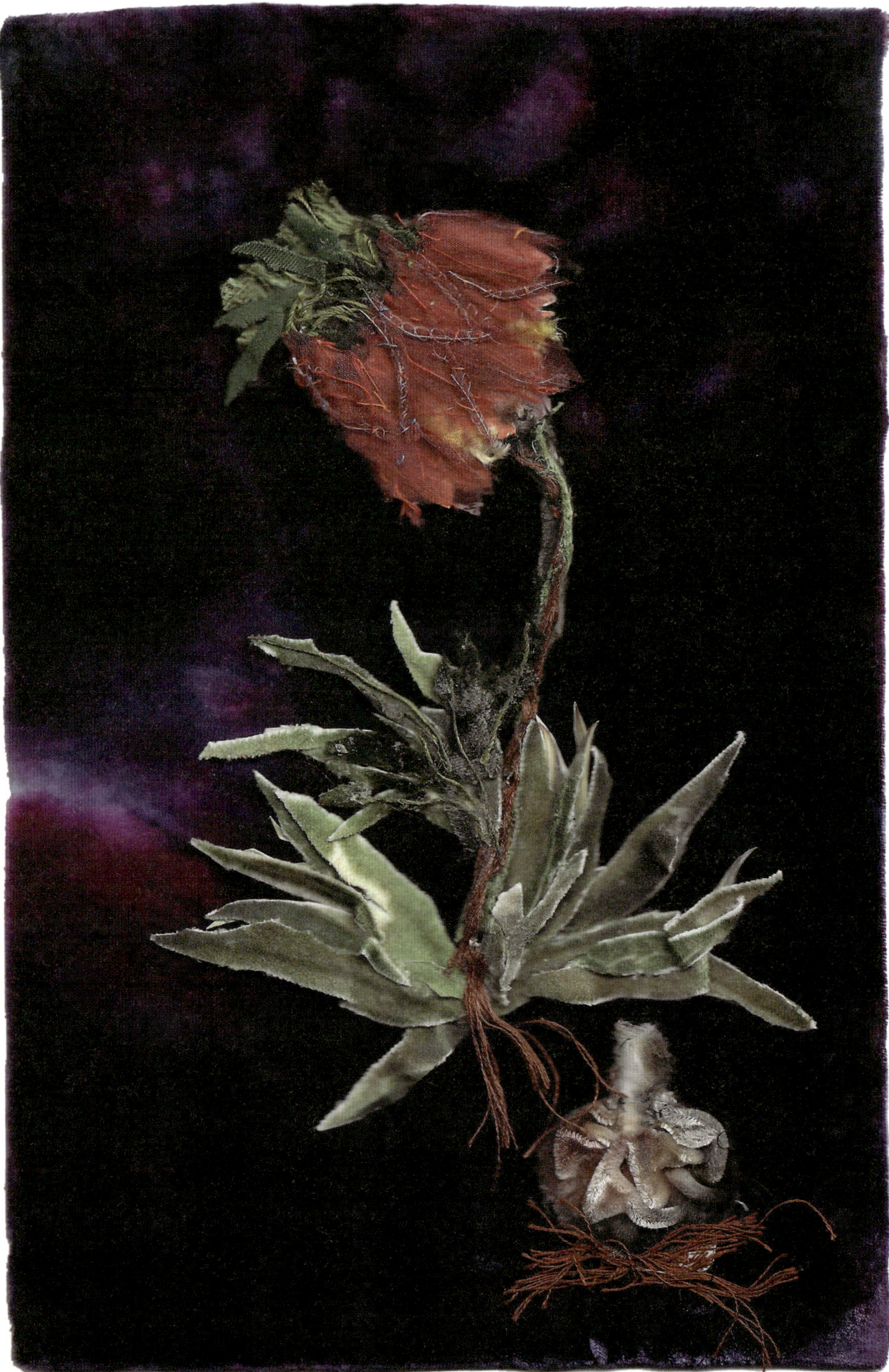

I was intrigued to find that fritillaria is rich with layers of symbolism and meaning across different cultures. It is mentioned in both Christian and Greek mythology in legends associated with humility or sorrow because of its weeping habit; in Iran, from whence the flower first came, it is a symbol of respect and remembrance.

In Great Britain, the Victorian Language of Flowers was much more specific. It gave a meaning to each type of fritillaria and stressed the importance of choosing the right variety of fritillaria to convey the right message, as serious consequences could otherwise happen.

This flower, in all its many forms, seems to have had the ability to conjure the imagination through the centuries and tell many stories.

One such storyline, which became a morality tale, is that the flowers of the Crown Imperial fritillaria, a much bigger and stronger variant than the fritillaria meleagris, were once pure white and grew in the Garden of Gethsemane on the Mount of Olives where Jesus was taken prisoner. While all the other flowers bowed their heads to show respect and obedience, the tall and bold Crown Imperial fritillaria, believing in the importance of its name, held up its head straight and firm. When Jesus asked it why it was doing this, the Crown Imperial blushed deeply with shame and hung its head and wept.

I chose to use the deep purple velvet as a background in this embroidery, as not only did the colour represent the penitential aspect of the story, but also, the contrast with the deep red silk of the flower petals was so beautiful.

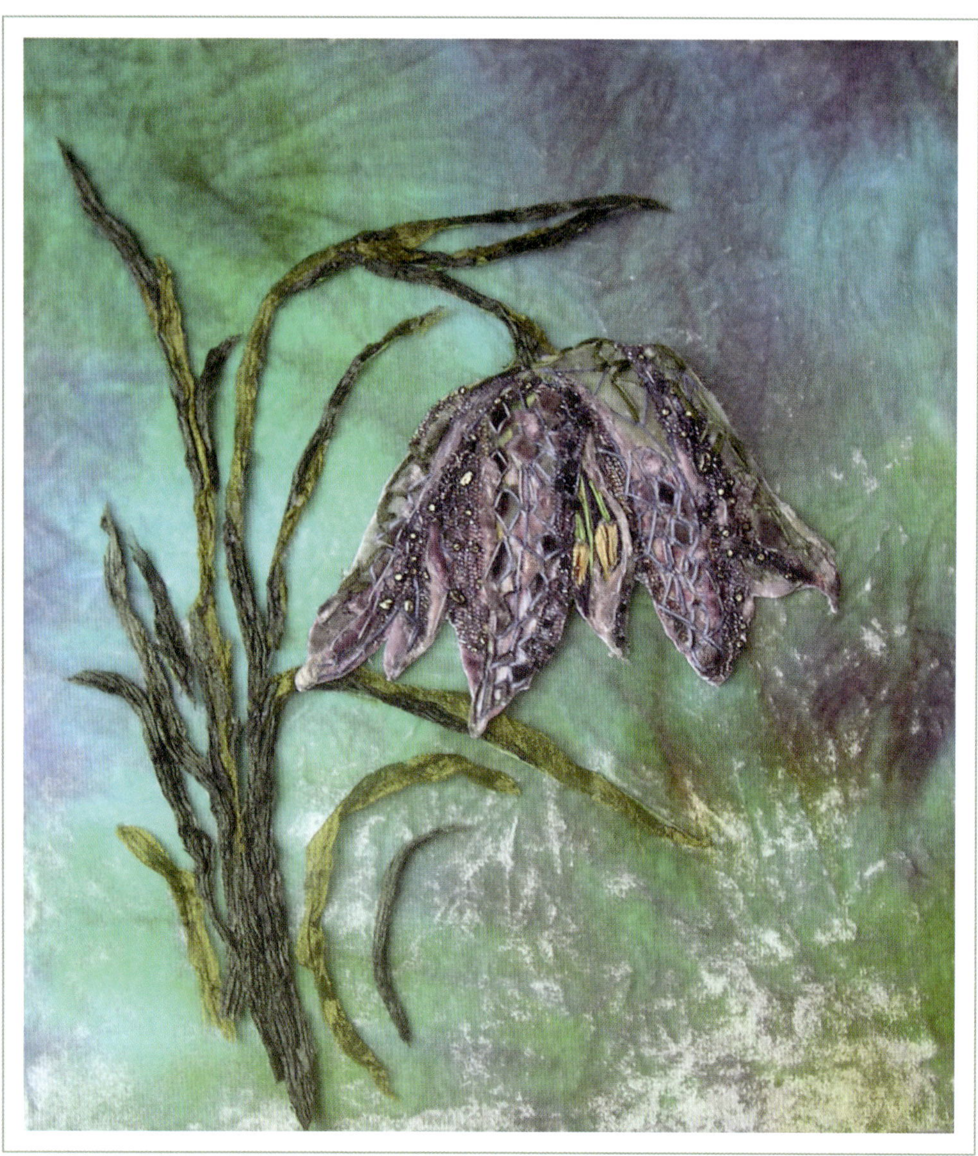

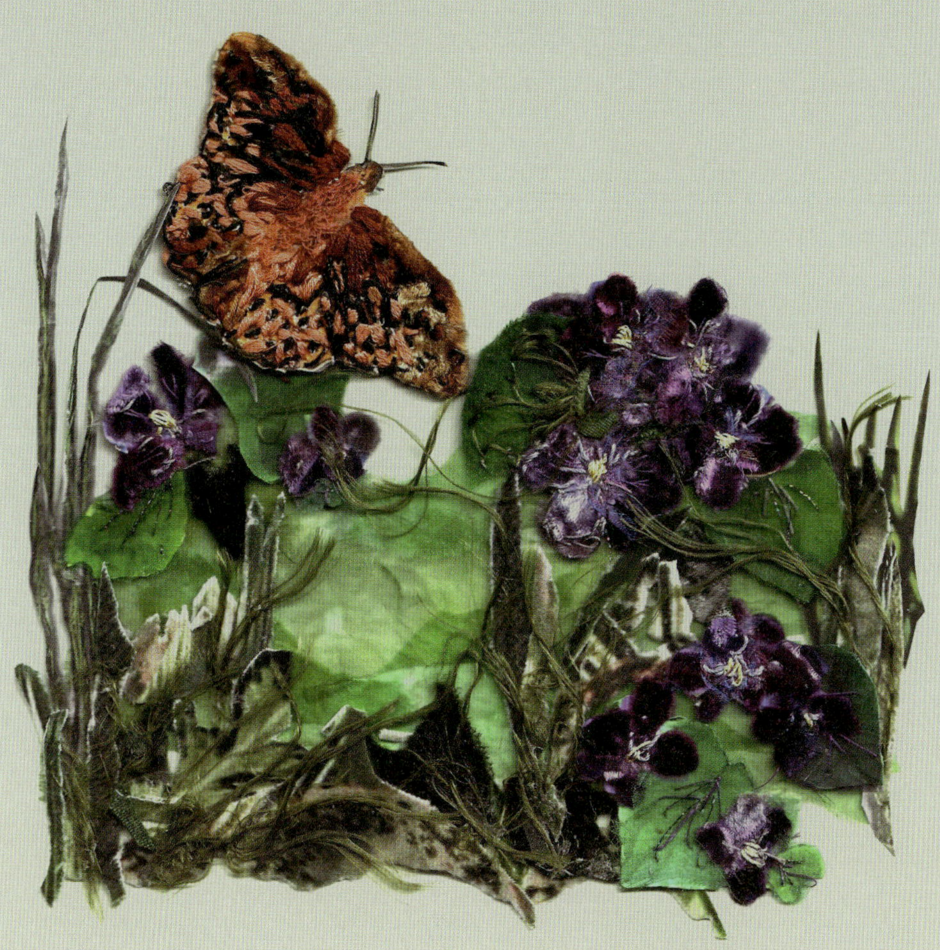

The fritillary butterfly, with its chequered marking, was named for the same reason as the flower. This lovely butterfly can be found in woodland glades, where it can be seen with its host plants, the violets that grow in the shade of the trees. The orange and amber of the butterfly seen with the deep purple of the violets being one of the colour glories found throughout nature. I stand there looking for as long as the moment will allow.

When I researched its medicinal properties, I found that species of fritillaria have been used in traditional Chinese medicine for over 2,000 years and are still used not only in China but also across the Himalayas and Southeast Asia. The products from the fritillaria are used mainly in therapeutic drugs for respiratory illnesses such as lung disease and asthma, but it is also used for minor ailments. As an example, I discovered this well-used and highly recommended recipe for everyday cough medicine.

Ingredients

15–20 Sichuan fritillaria bulbs
1 Chinese snow pear, hollowed out
Rock sugar, for sweetening

Method

Place the fritillaria bulbs inside the hollowed-out Chinese snow pear. Add a little sugar for sweetening. Steam the pear for 50 minutes. This produces a much-favoured home remedy for both children and adults.

Unfortunately for the plant itself, due to the sheer number of bulbs being used for successful medicinal purposes, many species of fritillaria are now endangered. In fact, remarkably, this beautiful plant has started to develop camouflage and change its colour in order to protect itself in heavily harvested areas. It has changed its normal jewel-like colours to grey or brown, blending in as best it can with its background, developing this disguise in an act of self-preservation in the areas where it is most under threat.

Late Spring

Buttercups and daisies scattered across rich pasture lands and meadows.

There are tall foxgloves with their spires of purple bells growing in the shade of the trees, and the garden is full of spring flowers, Persian carpets of wallflowers, tulips and forget-me-nots and I can smell the sweet scent of the wisteria flowering on my cottage wall.

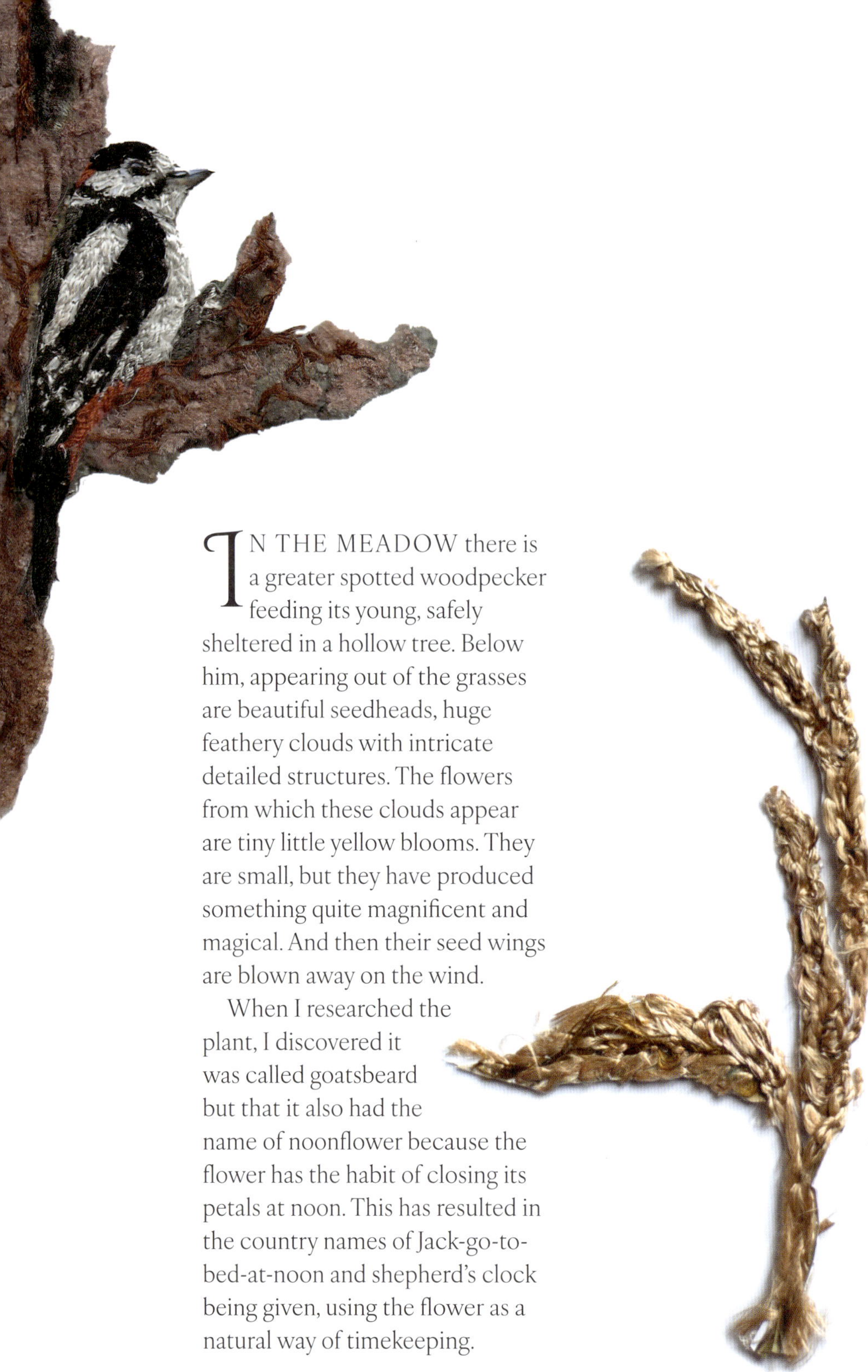

IN THE MEADOW there is a greater spotted woodpecker feeding its young, safely sheltered in a hollow tree. Below him, appearing out of the grasses are beautiful seedheads, huge feathery clouds with intricate detailed structures. The flowers from which these clouds appear are tiny little yellow blooms. They are small, but they have produced something quite magnificent and magical. And then their seed wings are blown away on the wind.

When I researched the plant, I discovered it was called goatsbeard but that it also had the name of noonflower because the flower has the habit of closing its petals at noon. This has resulted in the country names of Jack-go-to-bed-at-noon and shepherd's clock being given, using the flower as a natural way of timekeeping.

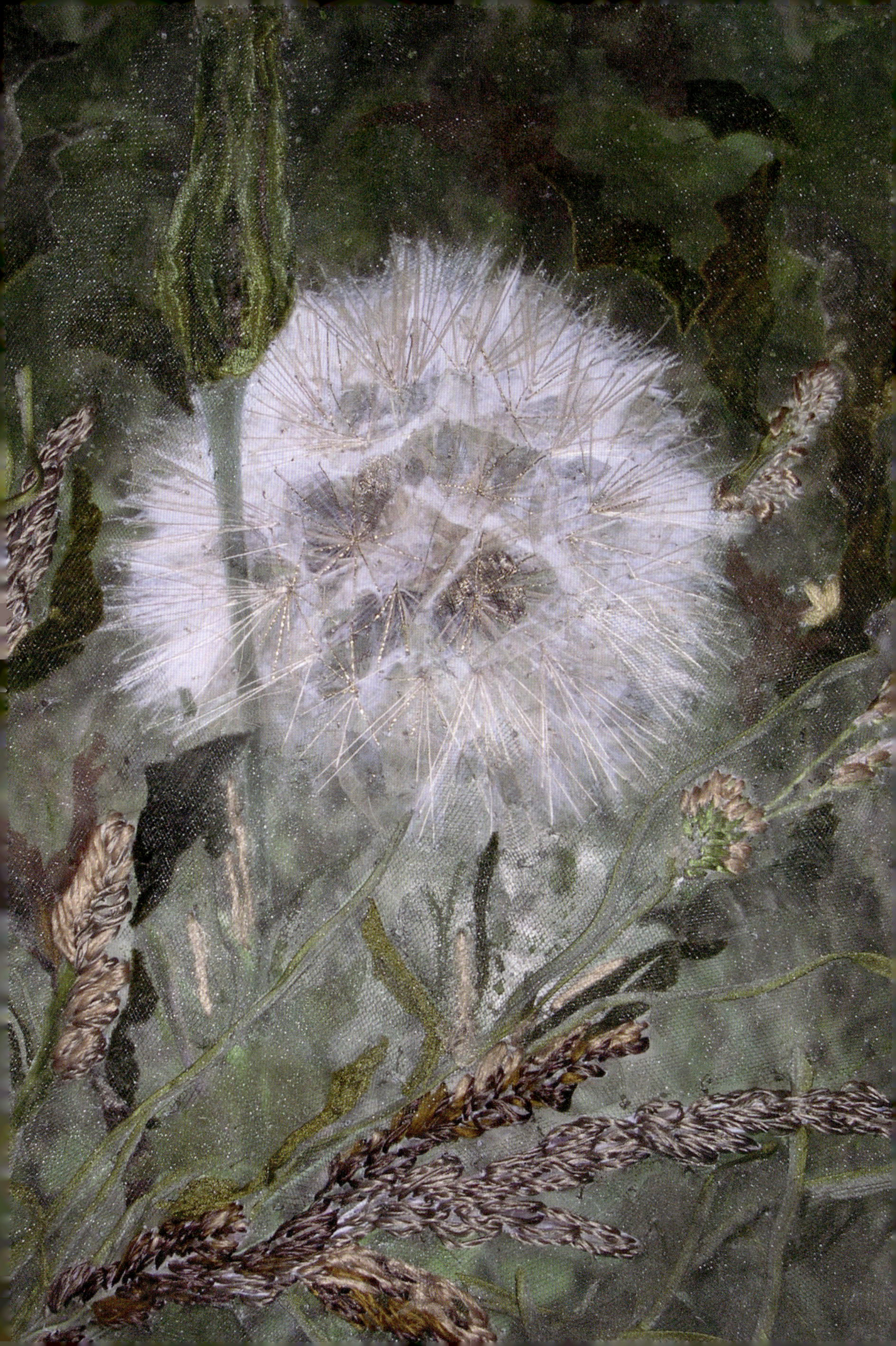

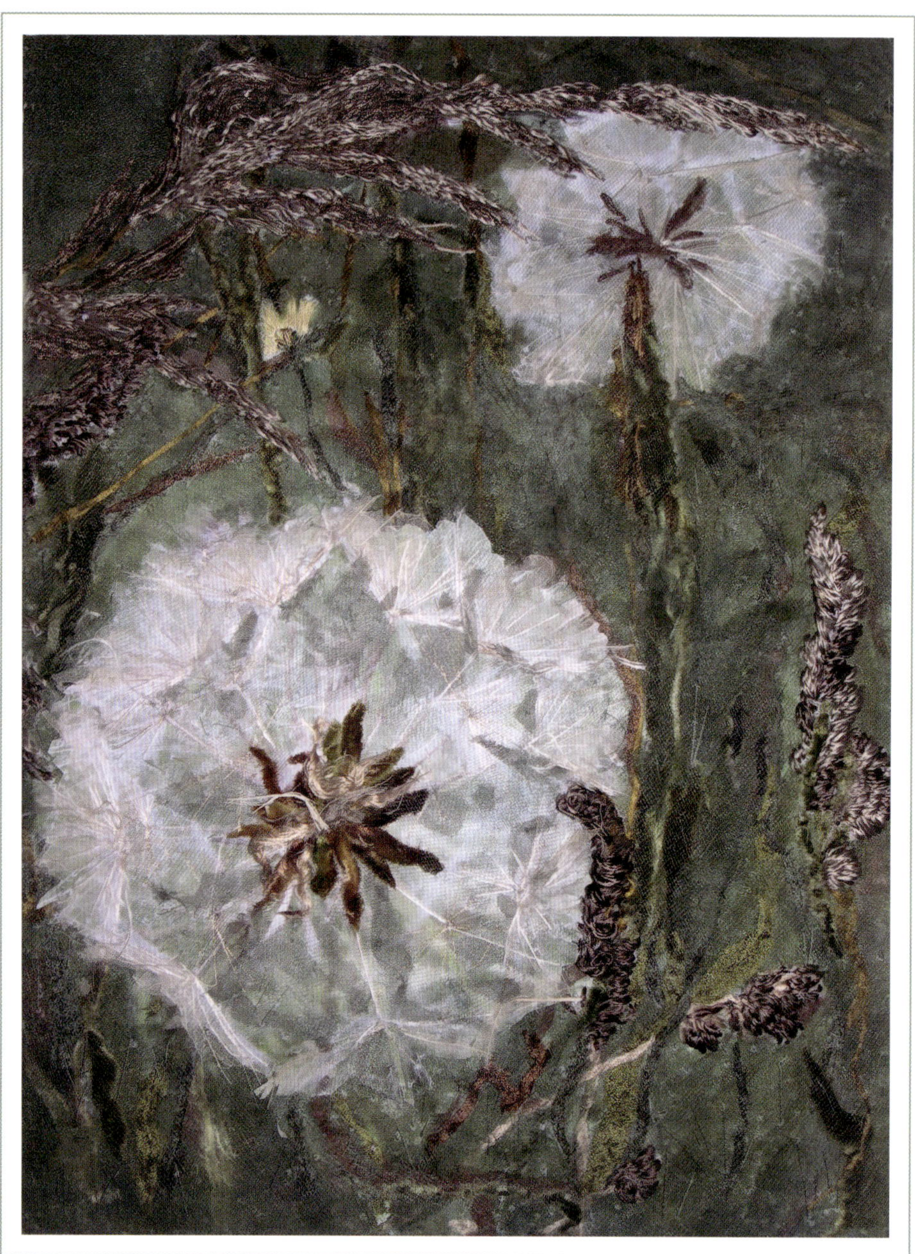

THE GOATSBEARD,
WHICH EACH MORN
ABROAD DOTH PEEP,
BUT SHUTS ITS FLOWERS
AT NOON AND GOES TO SLEEP.

Abraham Cowley

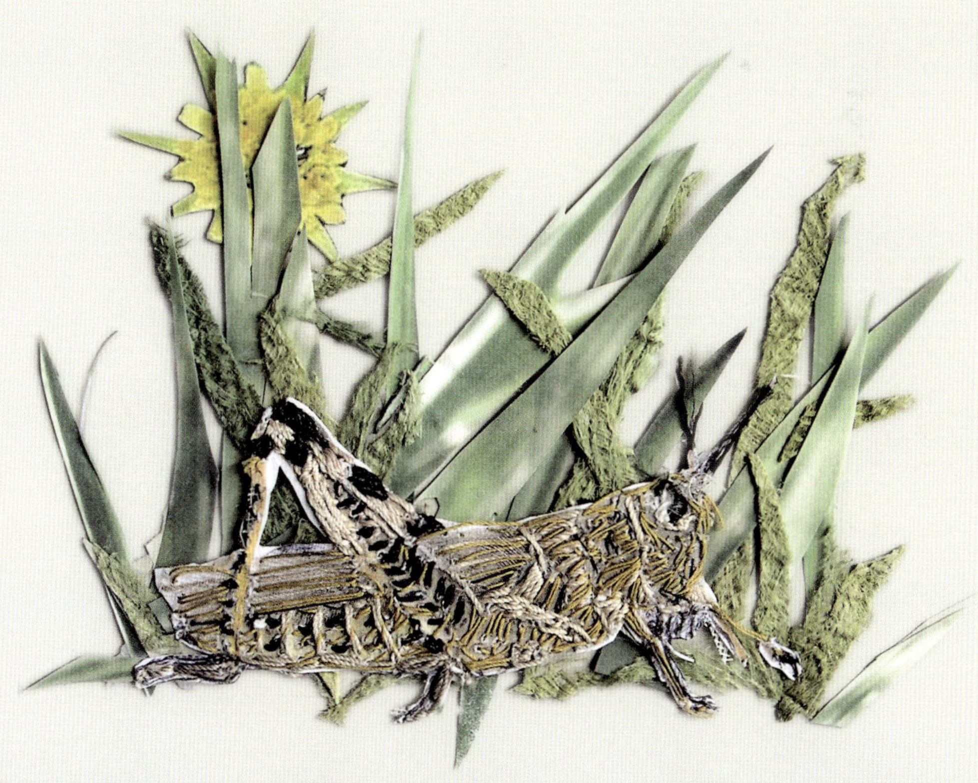

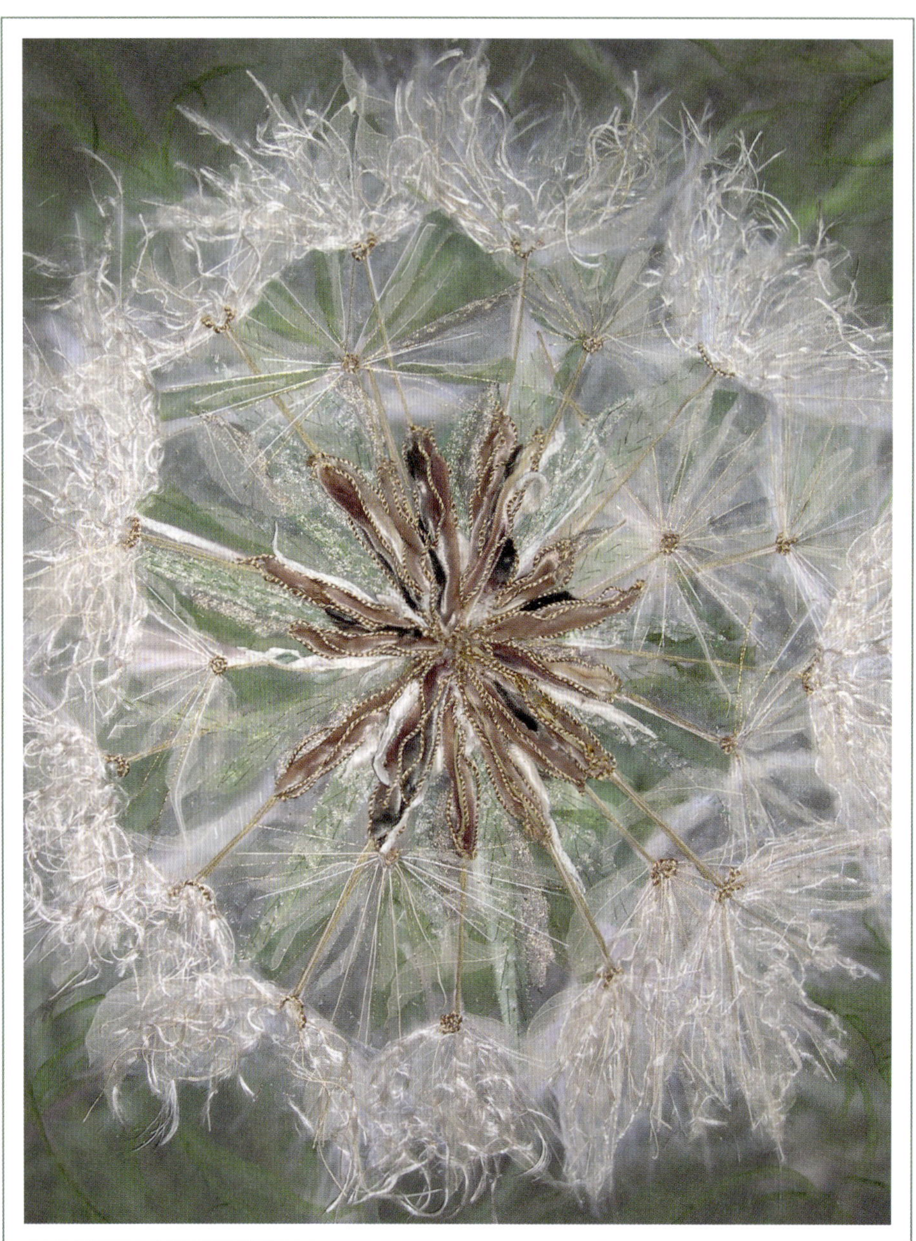

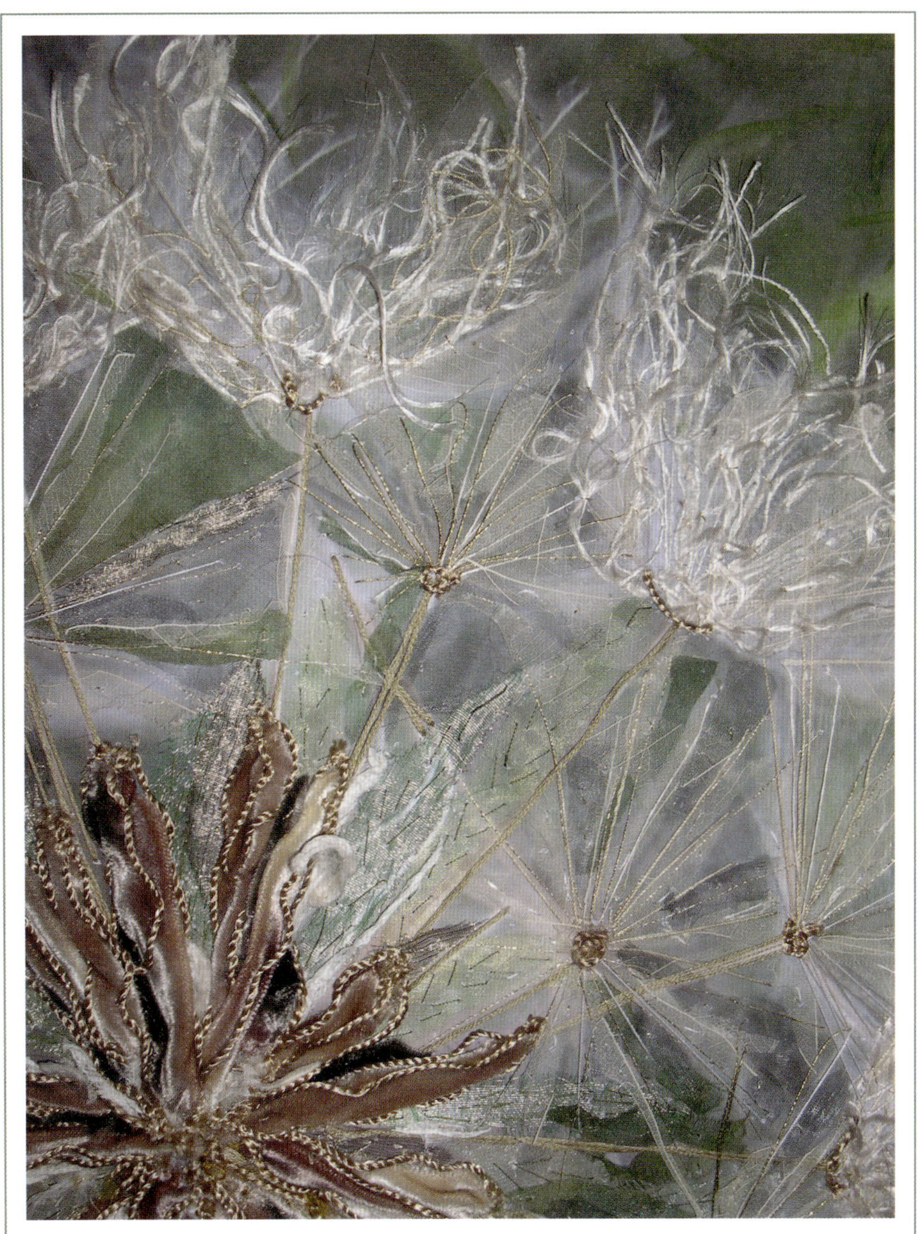

I wanted to discover more about this little wildflower with such a big heart. It is called goatsbeard because the beautiful large balls of feathery white seeds supposedly resemble the silky beard of a goat. I echoed that silkiness in the embroideries by using the finest threads, to bring its name to life. Selenite was the crystal I chose to accompany it, with its connection to the light of the moon, as the seedhead reminded me of sun, moon and stars.

Goatsbeard is sometimes also called meadow salsify, as it belongs to the same family as the vegetable salsify and in fact forms part of the Cretan diet. This diet has now become well known for its health-giving benefits because of its significant use of these 'wild greens'.

This recipe, for example, recommends the goatsbeard as a healthy and savoury addition to any meal that will help nourish the body.

Ingredients

10–15 thin goatsbeard stems, with flowers and leaves
1 onion, thinly sliced
Butter or oil to fry

Method

Sauté all ingredients over a low heat until the onions are clear and the goatsbeard has softened. Serve immediately.
Simple but tasty.

Another part of its story is that, as with many such plants, it not only formed part of a healthy diet but was also used for medicinal purposes. Culpeper included its use in his *Complete Herbal*. There are many recommendations. The poulticed root was applied to bee stings, and a tea made from the roots was used to stop bleeding and to treat stomach pains. Native Americans are renowned for their medicinal plant knowledge, and goatsbeard is still used in their present-day practices; they also use infusions from the roots for a variety of ailments including rheumatism, fever and blood disease. As with all their herbal remedies, they try to pick every third plant only, to prevent overharvesting.

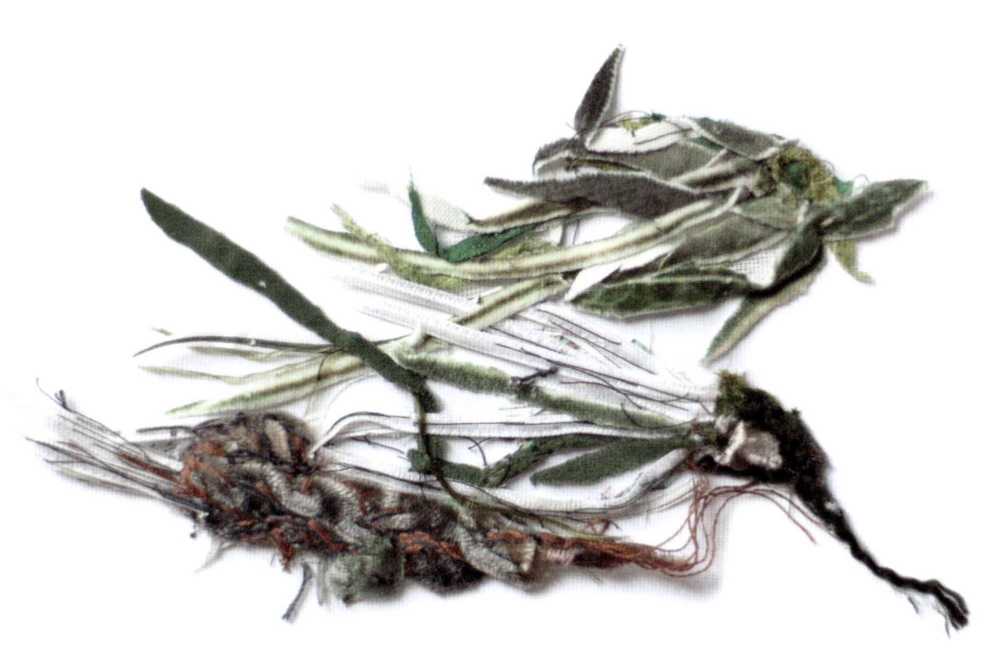

THE PASTURE GLEAMS AND GLOOMS
'NEATH BILLOWING SKIES THAT SCATTER AND AMASS.
ALL ROUND OUR NEST, FAR AS THE EYE CAN PASS,
ARE GOLDEN KINGCUP-FIELDS WITH SILVER EDGE
WHERE THE COW-PARSLEY SKIRTS THE HAWTHORN-HEDGE.
'TIS VISIBLE SILENCE, STILL AS THE HOUR-GLASS.

DEEP IN THE SUN-SEARCHED GROWTHS THE DRAGON-FLY
HANGS LIKE A BLUE THREAD LOOSENED FROM THE SKY: —

'The House of Life: 19. Silent Noon', Dante Gabriel Rossetti

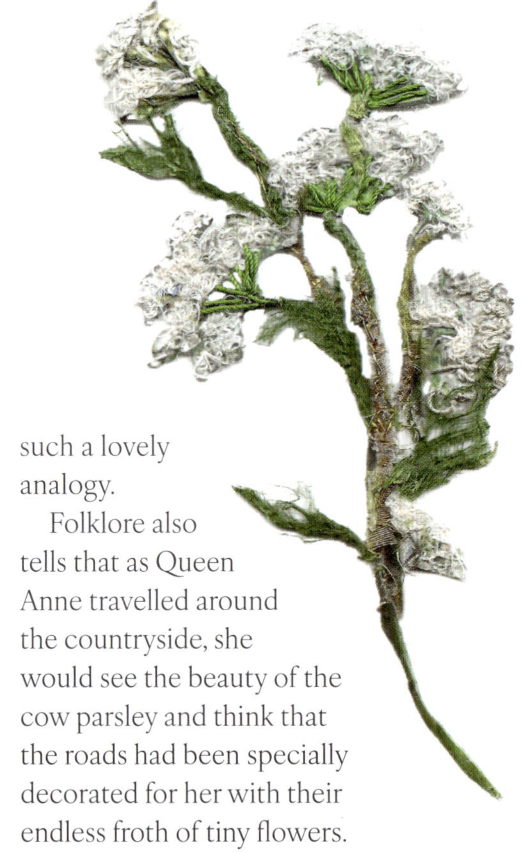

Late spring, and cow parsley is covering every square inch of woodland and meadow in its beauty. With the May trees also in flower, the lanes and fields are filled with blossom from sky to earth.

Cow parsley has many country names, such as wild chervil, fairy lace and Queen Anne's lace. This last name came from a folk tale that the flowers would bloom for Queen Anne and her ladies-in-waiting and echo the delicate lace they wore. In the cow parsley fragment embroidery on the opposite page, I have carried on with this theme. I have portrayed the flower as a sliver of lace because I think it is such a lovely analogy.

Folklore also tells that as Queen Anne travelled around the countryside, she would see the beauty of the cow parsley and think that the roads had been specially decorated for her with their endless froth of tiny flowers.

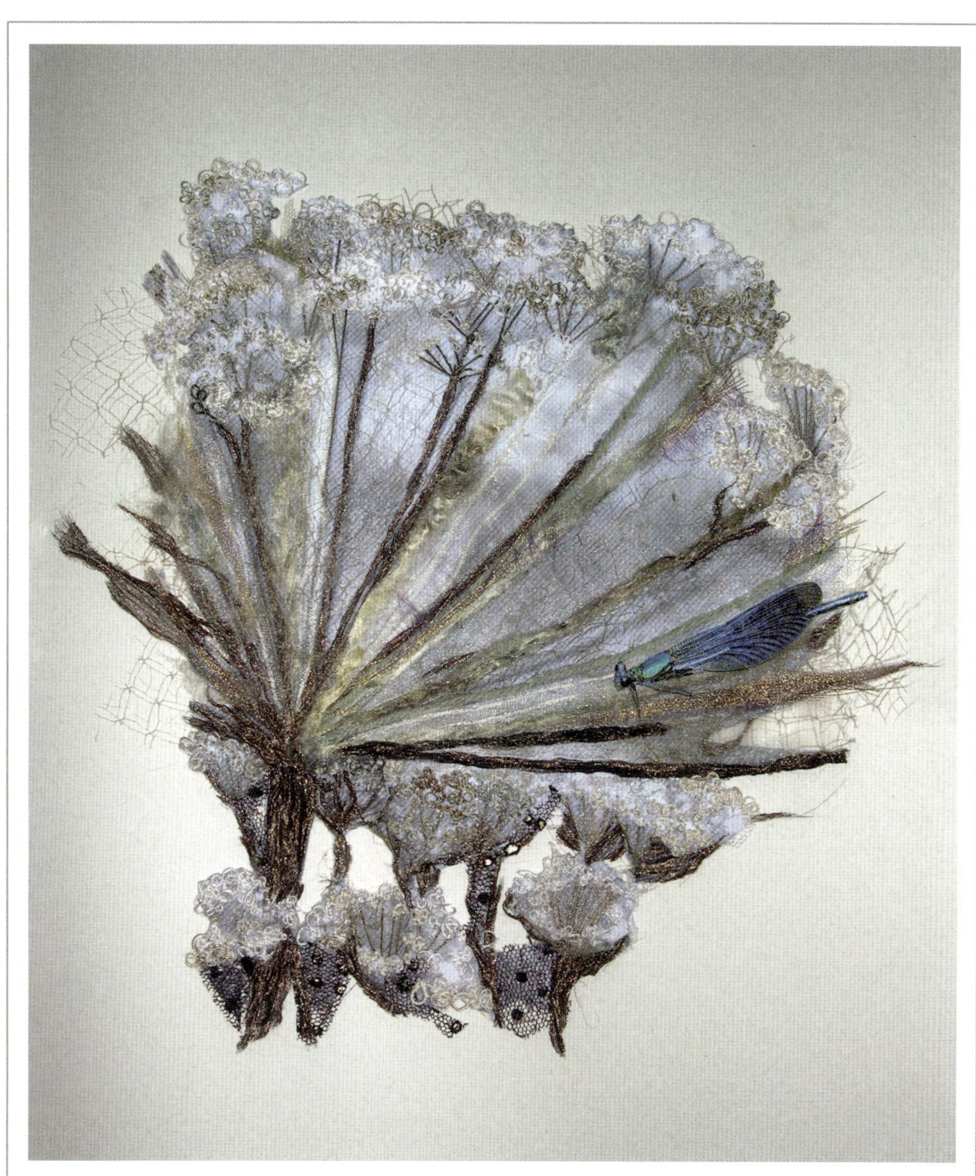

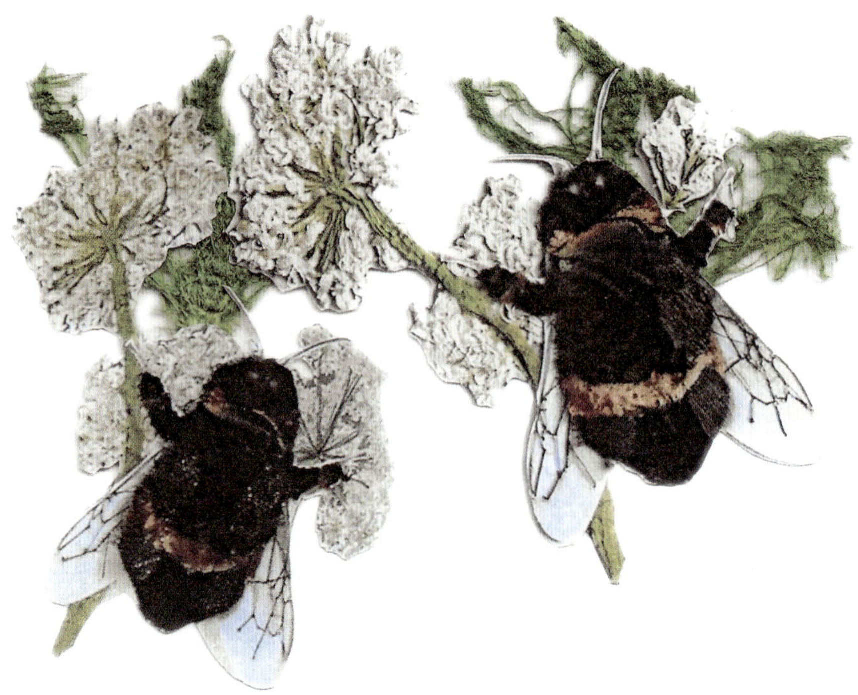

I placed peridot in the cow parsley embroideries as it is known as a stone of light and a gem of the sun, and it seemed fitting for the energy of such a lovely plant, flowering at the height of springtime.

Its abundance of tiny blossom umbels means this beautiful wildflower attracts a wide variety of insects. And all these insects are joyful subjects to embroider.

Bees and hoverflies use cow parsley as an early pollen source; many moths use it as a food source, and it is a nectar source for both orange-tip and swallowtail butterflies. Bees are the main pollinators for such delicious crops as apples, strawberries, pears and peaches; butterflies pollinate mainly tasty vegetables and herbs, and moths are just happy to feed from whatever is available, which makes them very important to the food world.

I had always thought of bees and butterflies as being the main pollinators, but recent studies have shown that moths also play a hugely active part in this life cycle, but have been undervalued purely because most of their work is done out of sight. You see the fat bumble bee buzzing lazily along; the moth tends to be much less visible.

Moths, being mainly nighttime insects, do not need bright colours to attract their mates. Although not as eye-catching as butterflies, I came to realise how very beautiful many of them are with their intricate patterning and subtle colours. Moths are notable for the hairiness of their bodies which holds most of the pollen they collect, making them very effective workers. But this fuzz is also wonderfully designed to act as a block against predators such as bats, which use echolocation to find their prey. The hairs on the moth are classified as a type of scale and help to block the sound waves, which makes them a most ingenious design feature.

The puss moth embroidered here shows the depths of these layers of scales. I have left him unfinished on his linen background to show the process of bringing him to life.

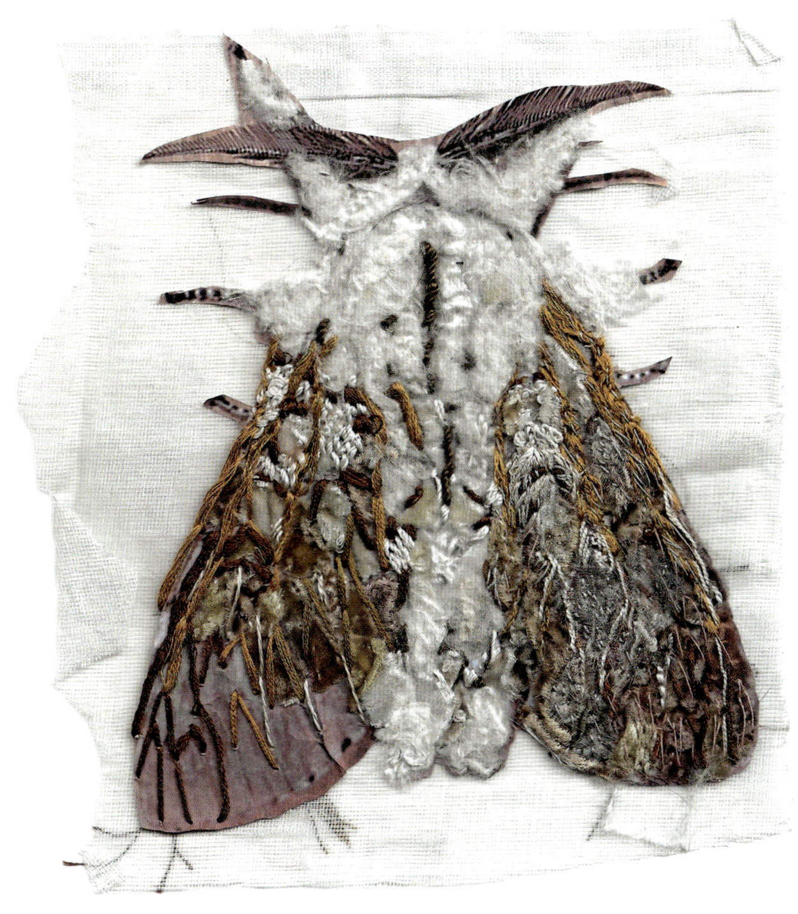

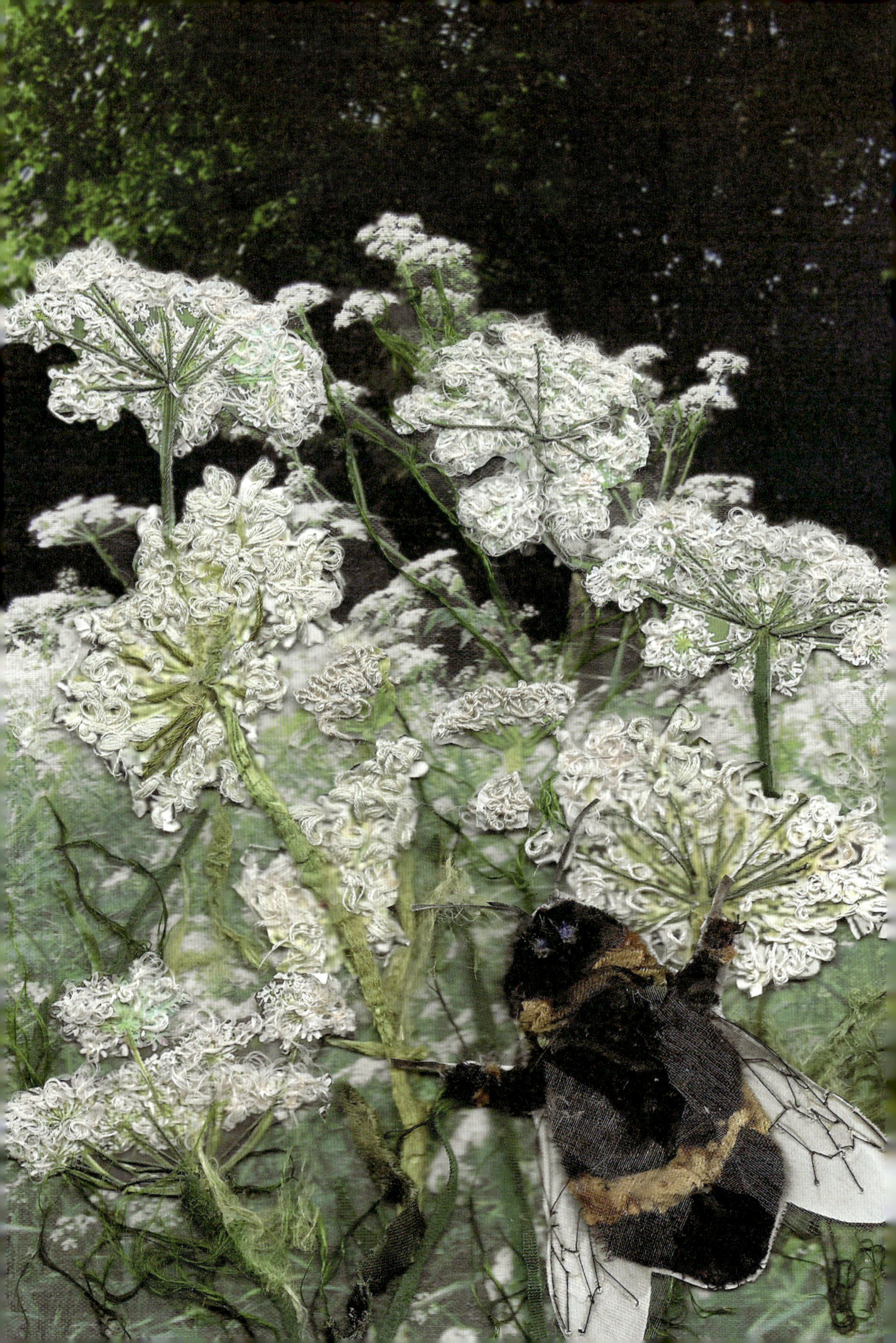

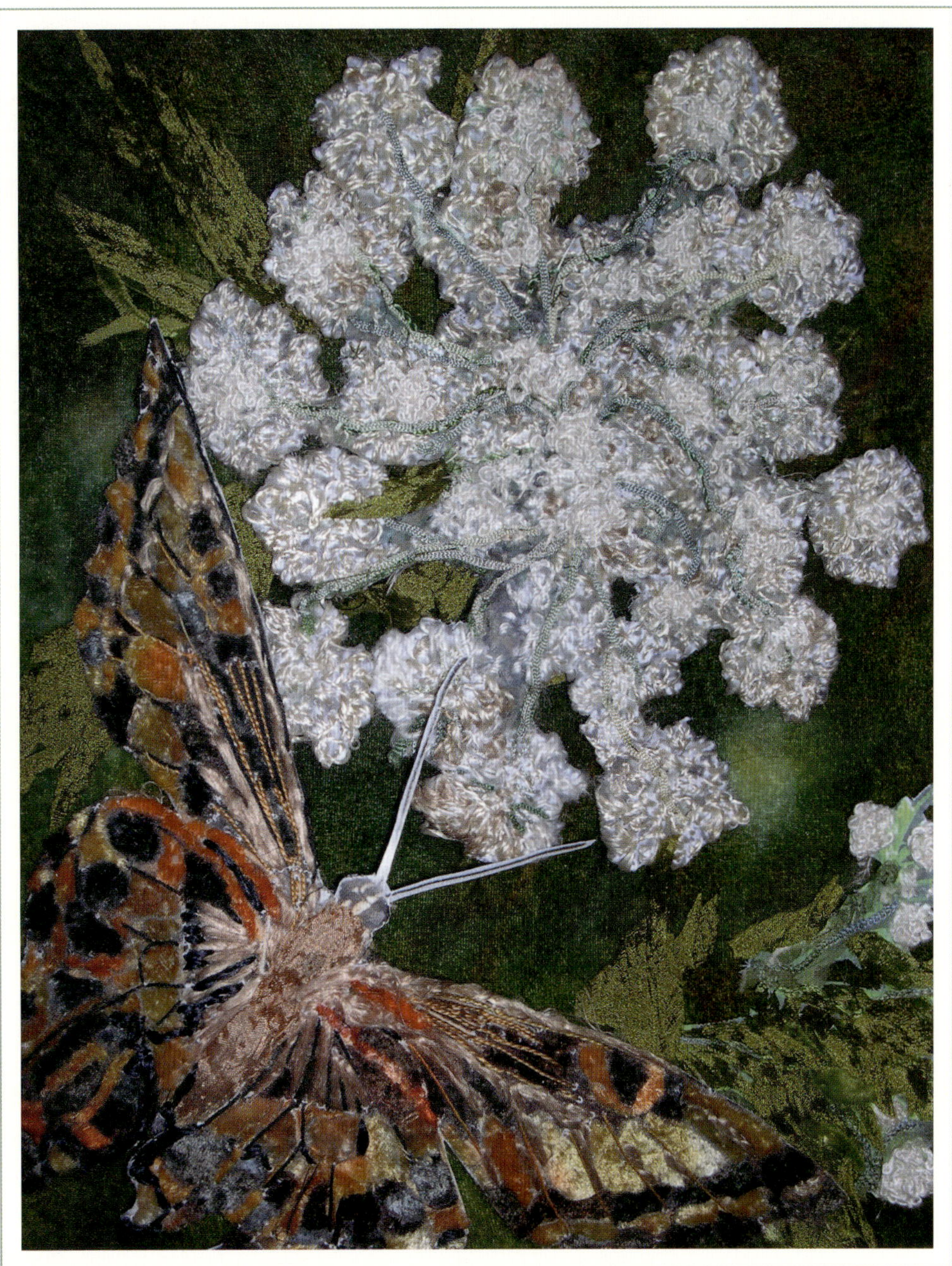

Cow parsley also has numerous health benefits for humans. It has been used in traditional medicines for centuries for minor illnesses as it has anti-inflammatory, antibacterial and antiseptic properties in its leaves and stems. Like the goatsbeard, cow parsley can be foraged as a 'wild green'. It has a mildly spicy flavour, and its leaves and roots can be used cooked or as a garnish or seasoning, but it is important to make absolutely sure that you are using cow parsley. Hemlock, very similar in appearance, grows in the same habitat and is deadly! For this very good reason, using cow parsley as a foraged food, although tempting, is best avoided.

Importantly, though, researchers at the University of Padua looking for a source of the lignin that forms a starting compound for several anti-cancer drugs, discovered that the entire cow parsley plant is a source of a very similar compound, with the highest concentration being in the roots. Studies in South Korea have shown that this substance is effective in treating cervical carcinoma cells. Chinese medicine also uses the dried roots to stimulate the production of red blood cells.

So, this beautiful plant can help save lives.

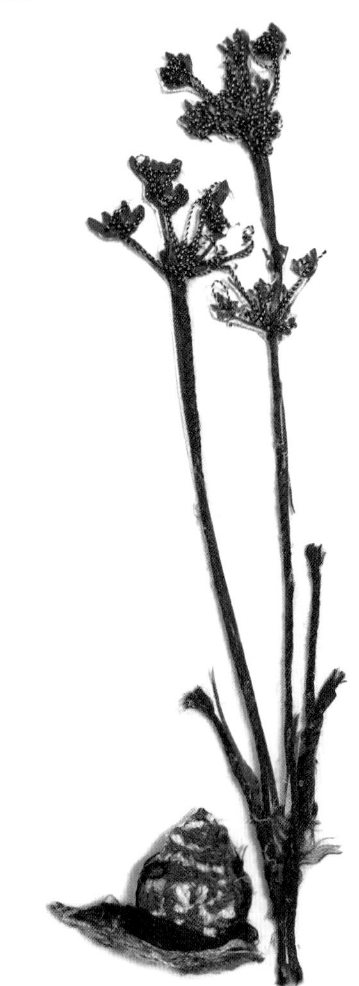

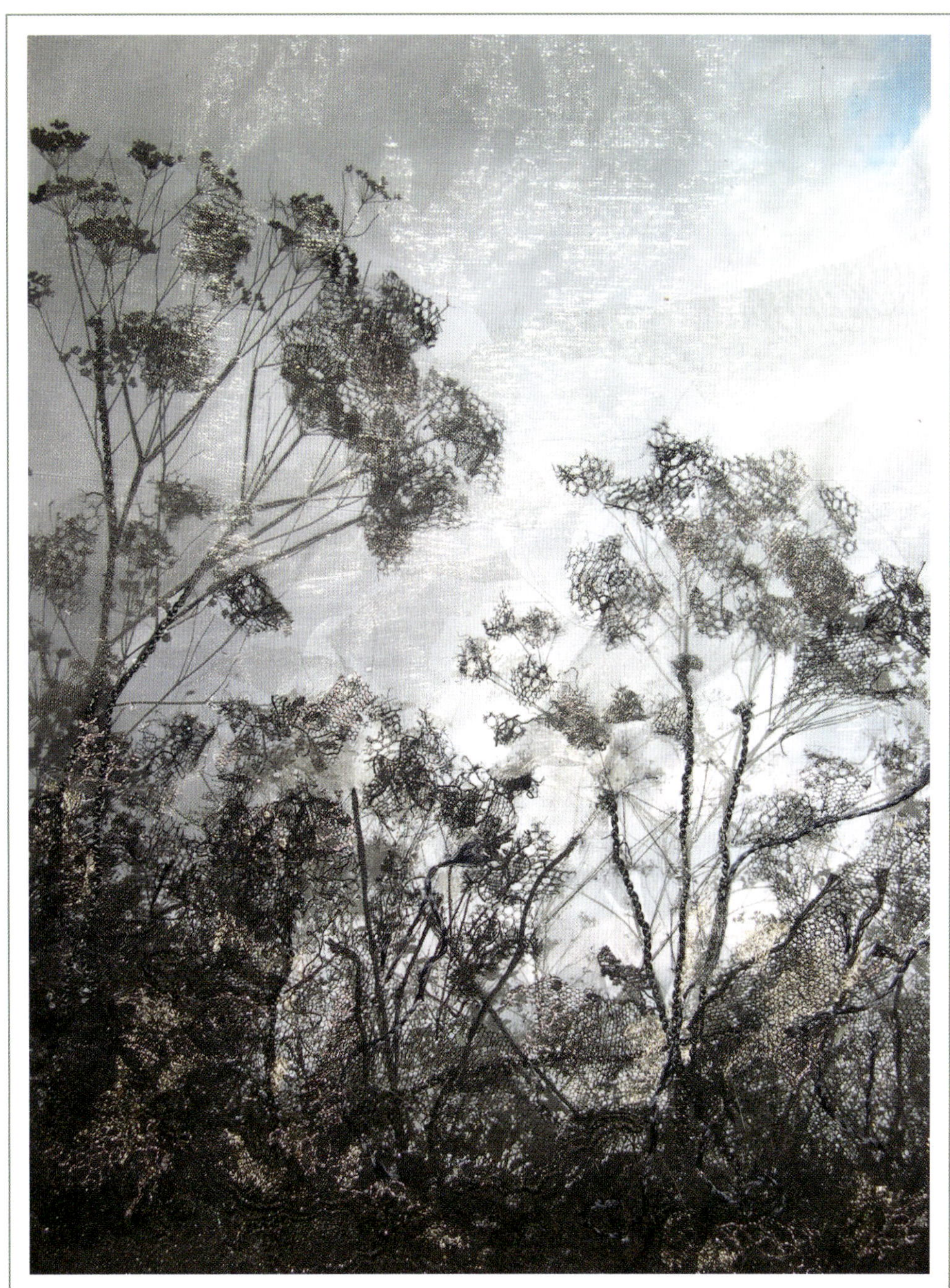

SUMMERTIME

High summer is the time for dreaming. Feeling the warmth of the sun, lying in the long grass and looking up at a perfect cloudless blue sky.

I always feel a sense of happiness and homecoming when I see bales of hay drying golden in the sun and the colour of the bleached grass in the fields. The path through the cornfields conjures up thoughts of childhood and lazy, hazy days helping with the harvest.

THE SUMMER DAYS are for dreaming; the summer nights are for enchantment. The nights are warm and welcoming on summer evenings, and the scent of flowers is still in the air. I created this daisy embroidery because I love to see the white flowers in the garden glimmering in the darkness, and this embroidery reminds me of those evenings. To add to the magic, in August, the light show of shooting stars puts on its dazzling display if you are lucky enough to see them.

A favourite time for me is when pipistrelle bats perform aerobatics as the owls begin to call. There is that magical moment when the dusk becomes twilight and the bats suddenly emerge. D.H. Lawrence wrote about it when watching swallows over the river Arno: 'Look up, and you see things flying between the day and the night; Never swallows. *Bats!*'

I always go to the bottom of my garden to watch them. I never quite know if I have the timing right, but then, with a swoop, they are there.

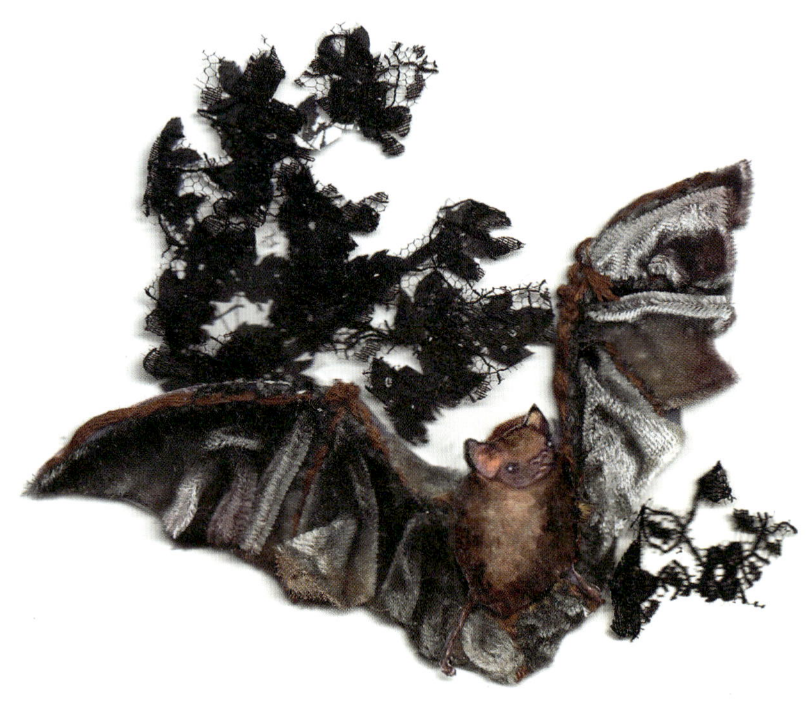

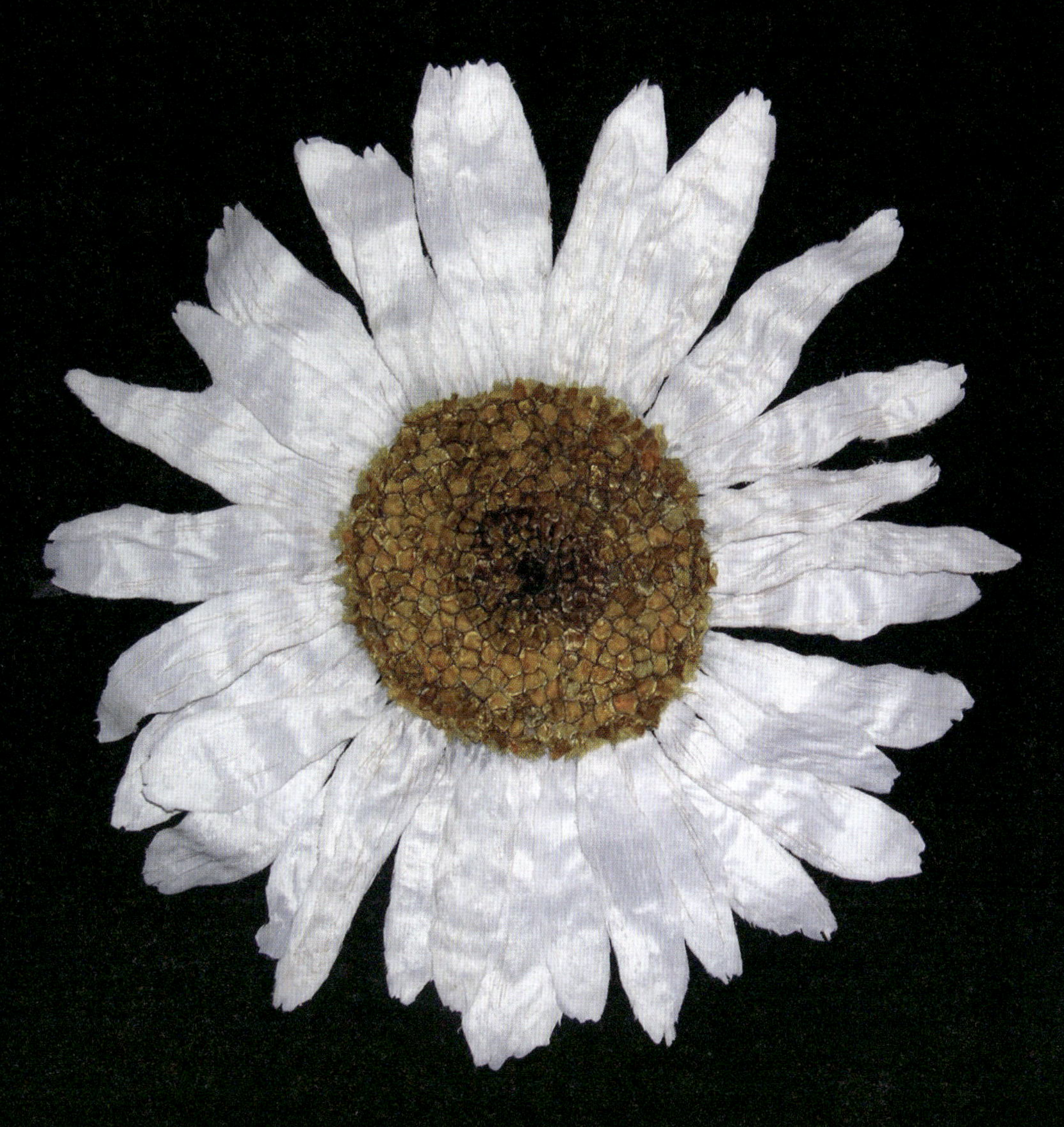

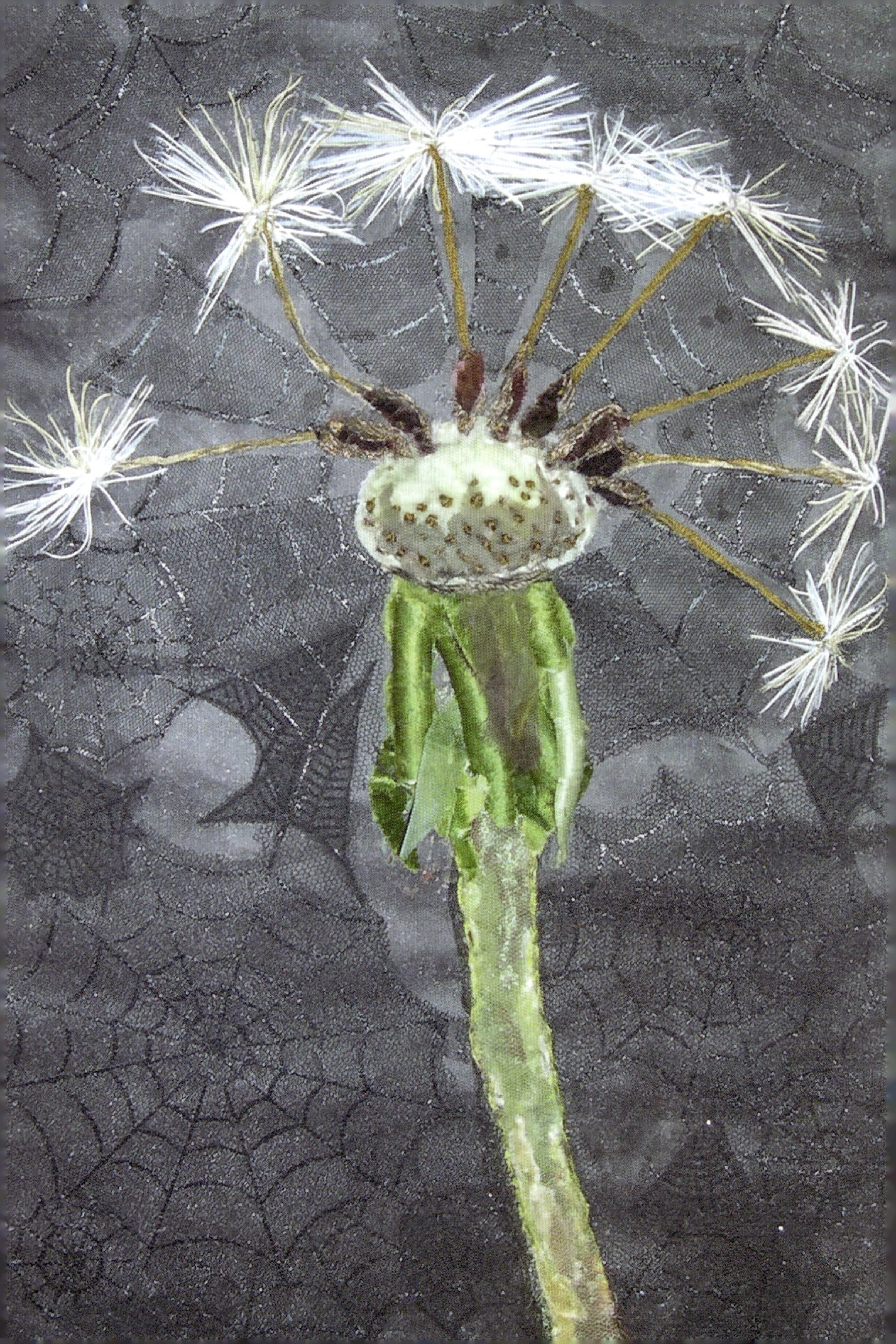

DANDELIONS – DANDELIONS!
I USED TO PASS YOU BY;
BENEATH MY FEET YOUR YELLOW STARS
I CRUSHED WITHOUT A SIGH;
I USED TO GAZE UPON YOUR BLOOMS
WITH BUT A CARELESS EYE,
AND IF OF YOU I THOUGHT AT ALL,
KNEW NOT THE REASON WHY.

Franklin Stanwood

The humble dandelion is also called the star flower, and I created these embroideries thinking of it as one of summer's shooting stars seen in a velvety night sky. Elusive as shooting stars are, the dandelion is the one star that is very easy to find.

The star flower is a very apt name for the dandelion, as in many ways it is a gift from the heavens. It has an immense number of medicinal qualities, is extremely useful for wildlife pollination and is an all round food for humans. It is found virtually everywhere and is nearly always in bright flower, which makes it an invaluable asset, even though gardeners might not agree. Dandelions could be one of the most under-recognised food sources we have with their abundance of nutrients and health benefits. They require nothing in return, as they are an entirely self-sufficient plant.

Every part of the dandelion is edible, from the roots to the leaves and flowers, even the unopened flower buds and stalks can be used, so there are numerous dandelion recipes for using every part of the plant, both for food and medicine. And the plant itself seems to flourish no matter how much it is harvested, happily propagating itself in every imaginable place.

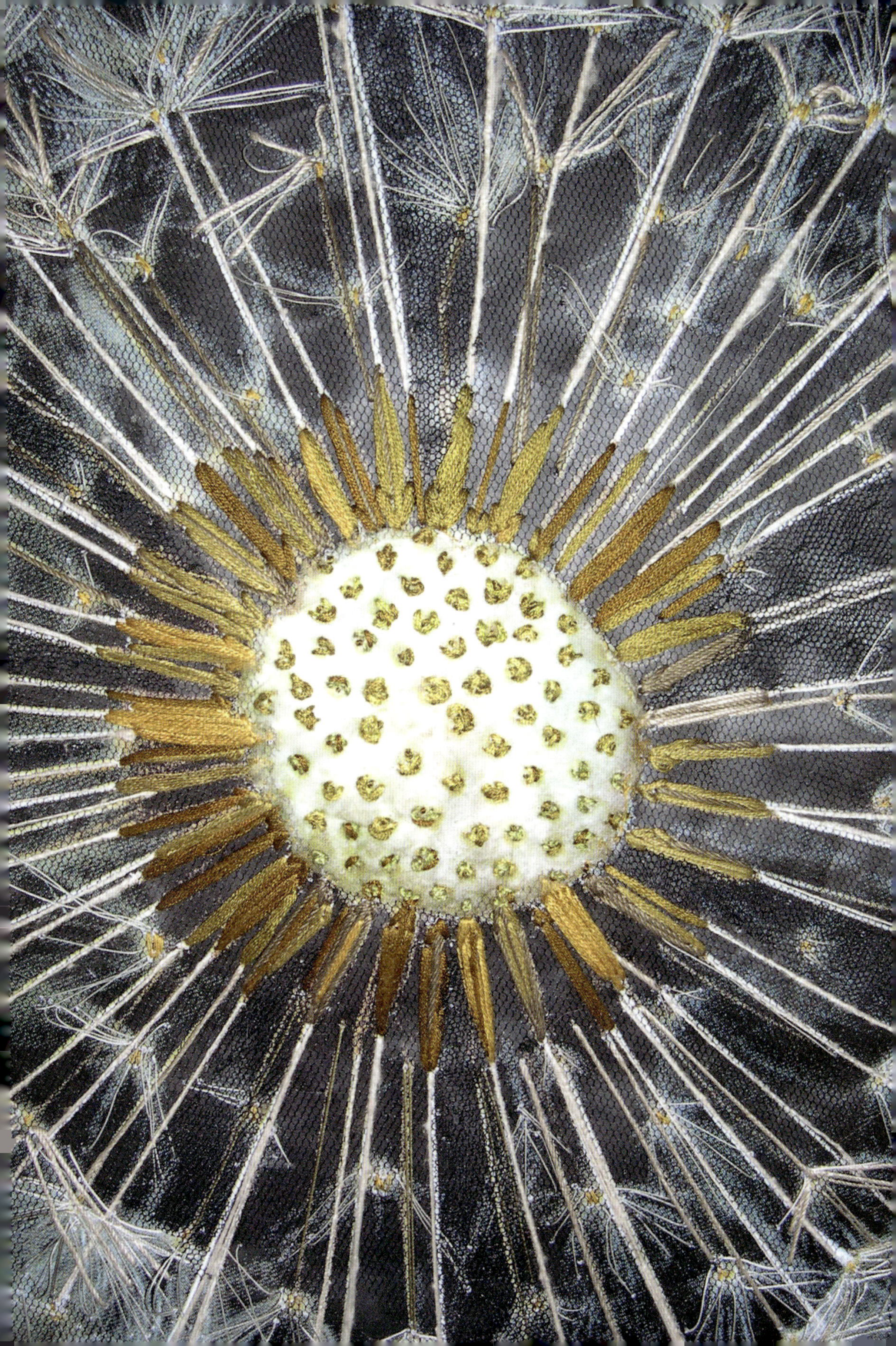

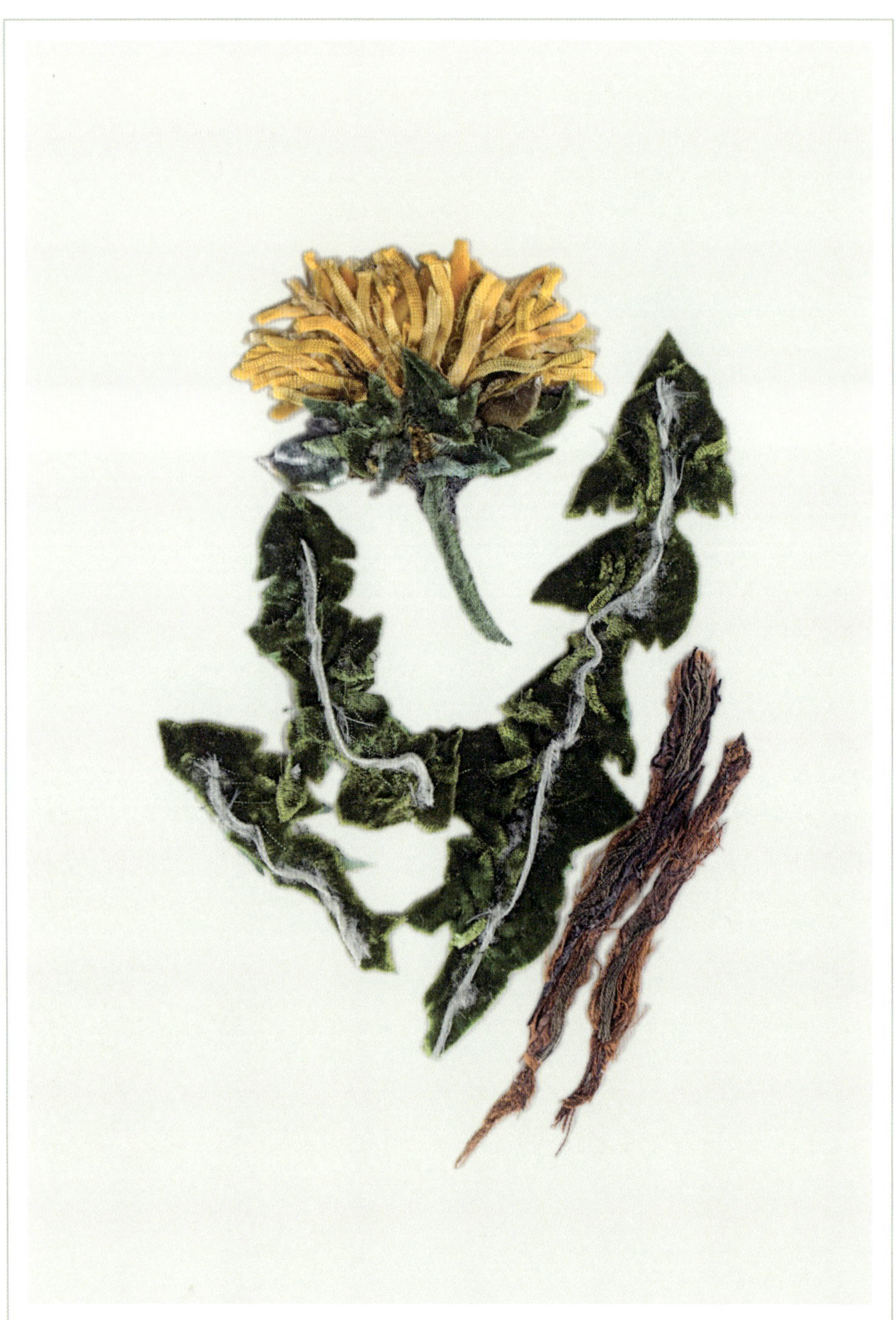

Dandelions are seen as a symbol for surviving hard times and perseverance, being a most persistent flower that never gives up, so dandelion tea is the tea to drink when feeling as if help is needed.

The benefits of dandelion tea vary with the part of the plant used. The flowers are high in antioxidants and are thought to help with alleviating pain. The leaves are rich in vitamins and minerals and are used to stimulate digestion and also as a diuretic. The root is used to support the liver. The tea can be made using the flowers, leaves or roots, simply steeping them in boiling water for ten or so minutes to produce a delicious and comforting brew, sprinkled with stardust.

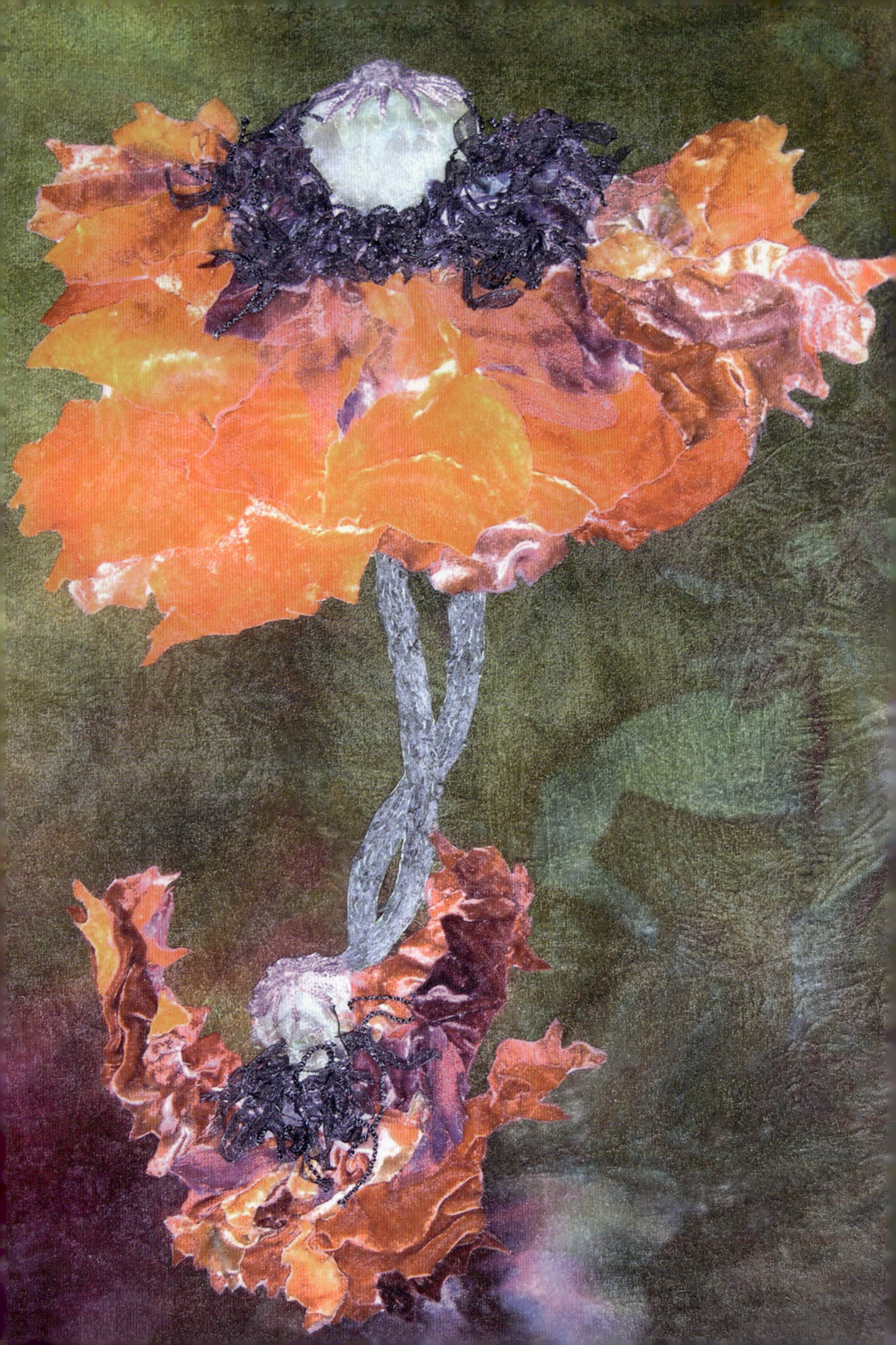

...LIKE A YAWN OF FIRE
FROM THE GRASS IT CAME,
AND THE FANNING WIND
PUFF'D IT TO FLAPPING FLAME.

Francis Thompson

This most beautiful oriental poppy flowered in my garden. It flowered with such complete abandon that every day I marvelled at it in all its glory of living crimson.

The embroidery is my lasting memory, created with the richest colours of velvets and threads to show its heart and soul, as befitting such a sumptuous flower, with a ruby at its centre.

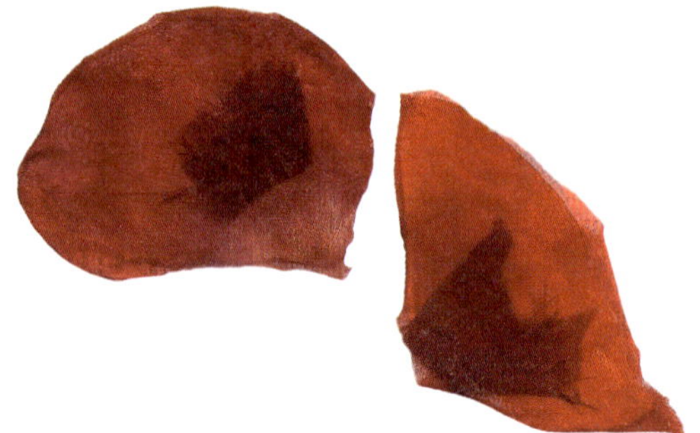

The poppy has many varieties, but all of them seem to be significant.

I think of the sight of a field poppy in its simplicity, but it is known worldwide for its association with the war dead because it was the only flower that would grow on the otherwise barren battlefields where so much disturbance and destruction and death had taken place. Following the publication of John McCrae's famous poem 'In Flanders Fields', there was a campaign for the poppy to become the symbol whereby the war dead would never be forgotten. I remember the amazing tribute at the Tower of London, which touched everyone who saw it, where the entire moat was filled with red poppies. I embroidered these fallen poppy petals for that same reason.

The poppy is linked with death in many ways, but it has also long been known for its medicinal benefits for the living.

Ancient Egyptian doctors had their patients eat the seeds of the opium poppy to relieve pain. The powerful alkaloids which are used today for vital painkillers such as morphine and codeine all come from the milky latex collected from the unripe seed capsules. The legend is that the poppy was created by the Greek goddess Demeter to ease her pain and allow her to sleep after the loss of her daughter Persephone.

Linking with this legend, poppies used on gravestones symbolise eternal sleep, but they can also offer hope as symbols of restful sleep and recovery and resurrection. The poppy was prized so highly for these reasons in ancient Egypt that, along with magnificent treasures, Tutankhamun was entombed with embroidered ceremonial clothing made partly from poppy plants and with illustrations of this lovely flower on his jewellery and furniture. This seems to have been done with tender concern for the boy king's comfort in the afterlife.

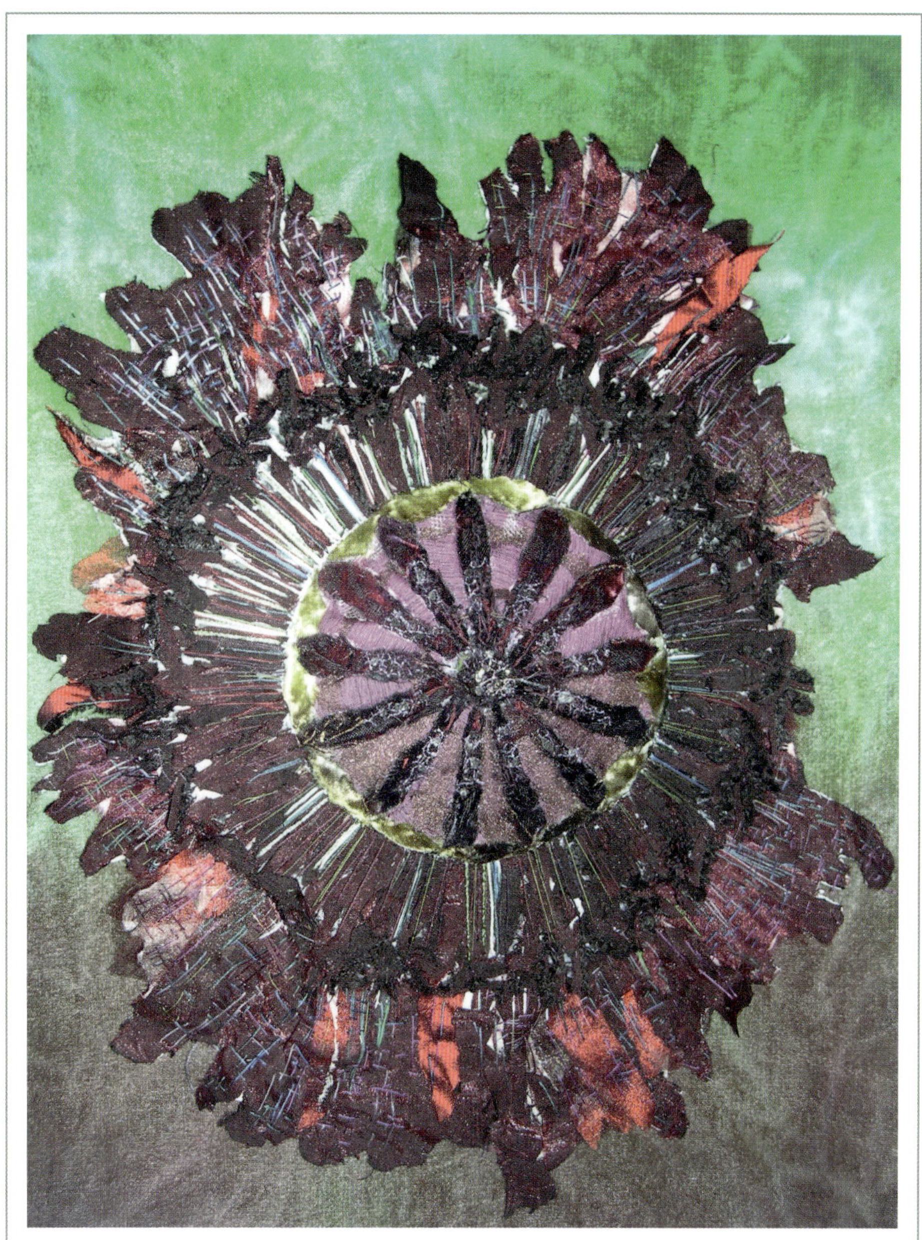

I wanted to include this embroidery of the Camberwell Beauty butterfly because its colouring is so perfectly suited to the poppy, and because the embroidered caterpillar gives hints of the glory that it is to become. The Camberwell Beauty butterfly is not native to the British Isles, but it has been sighted here in gardens in the month of August where it likes to feed from summer garden flowers and overblown fruit.

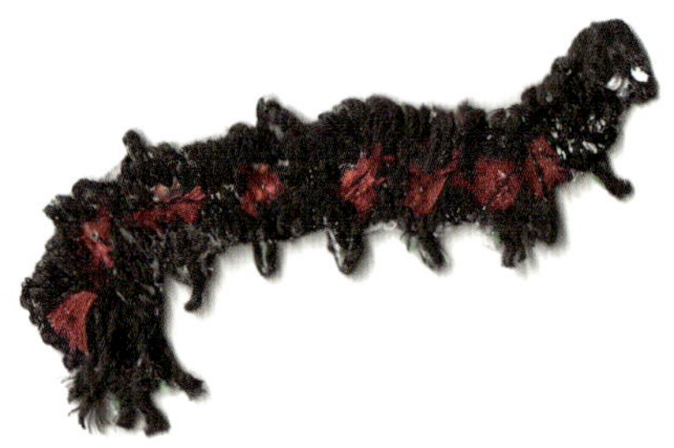

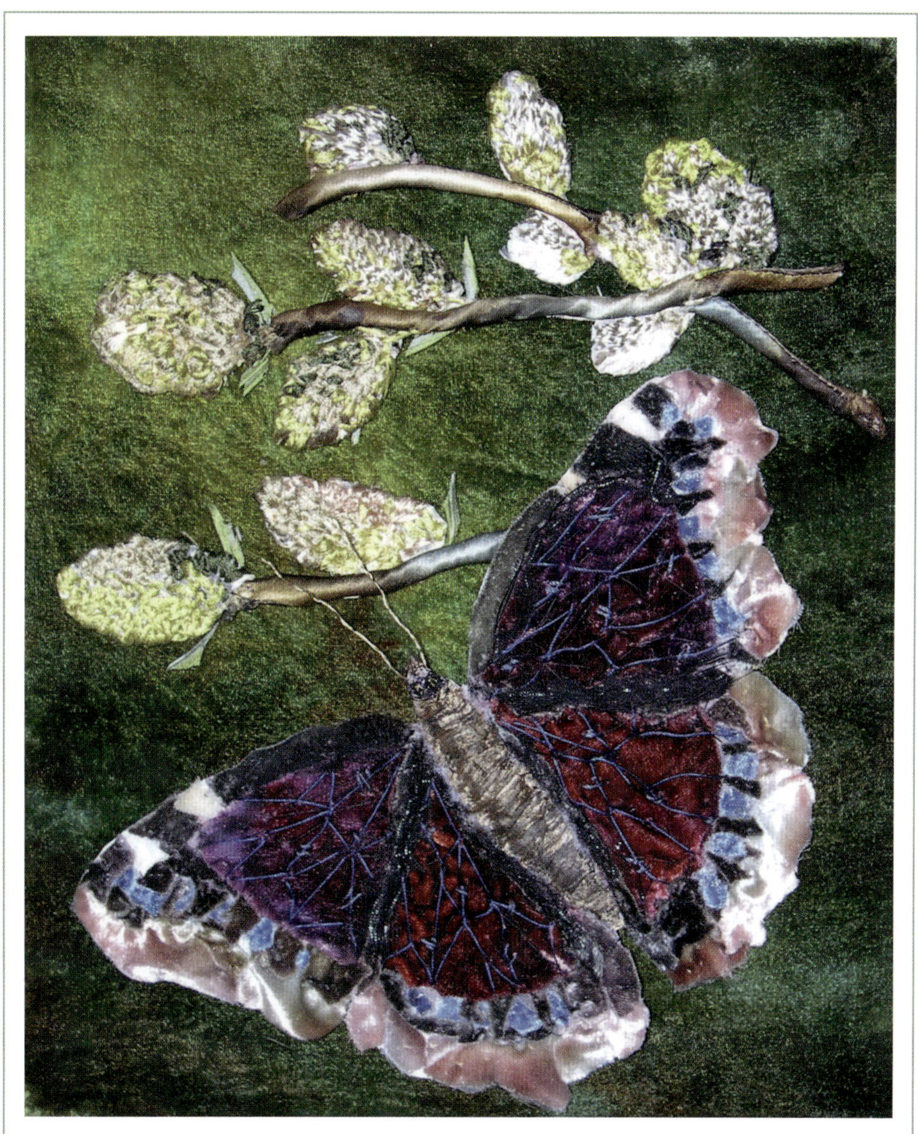

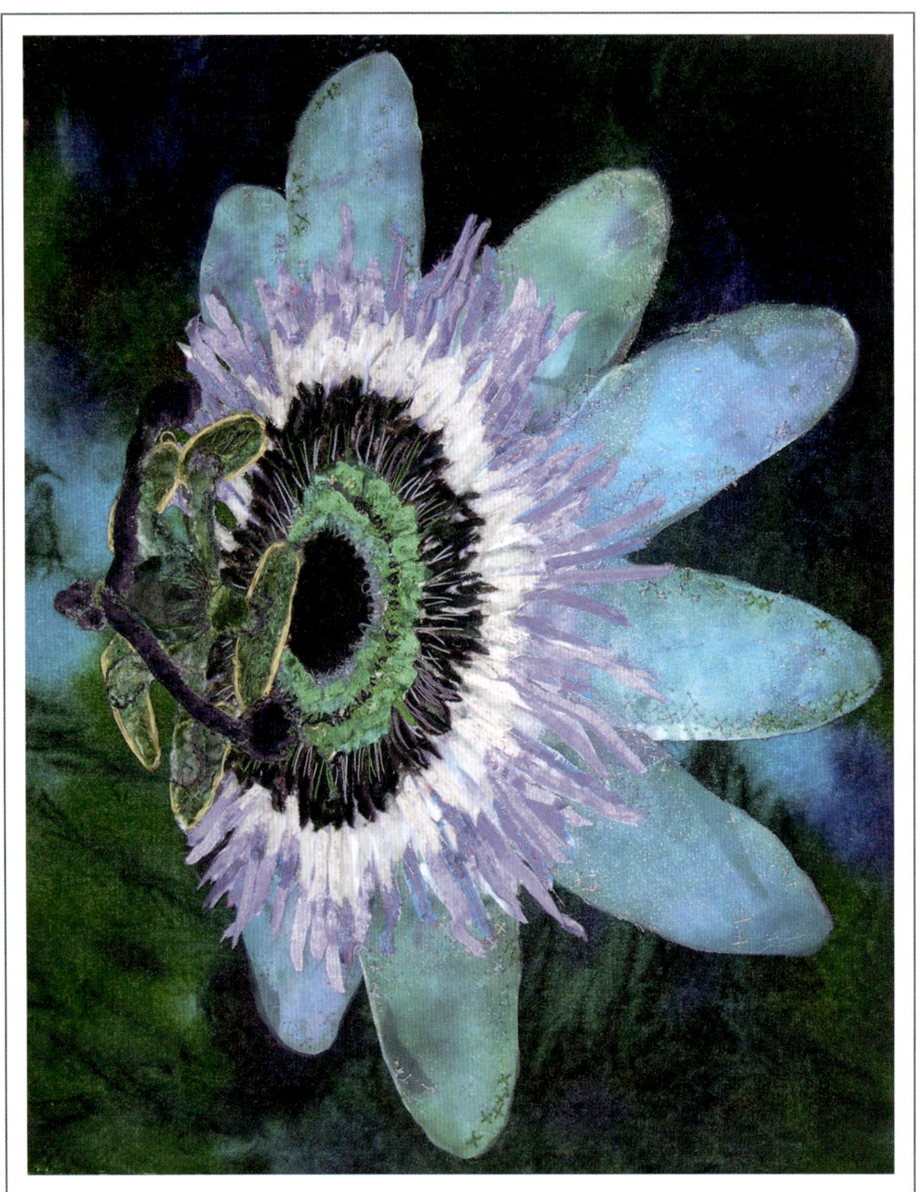

...SHE HEARD NO SOUND BEYOND HER GATE,
THOUGH VERY QUIET WAS HER BOWER.
ALL WAS AS HER HAND HAD LEFT IT LATE;
THE NEEDLE SLEPT ON THE BROIDERED VINE,
WHERE THE HAMMER AND SPIKES
OF THE PASSION-FLOWER
HER FASHIONING DID WAIT...

'The Ride to the Lady', Helen Gray Cone

The legend is that the passion flower was the first flower sixteenth-century missionaries saw when they set foot in the Amazon region of Brazil. They saw it as a sign of good fortune for their mission, as the parts of the flower seemed to resemble the Passion of Christ.

The three lobed leaves represented the spear that pierced His side. The tendrils represented the scourge or whip. The corona at the centre of the flower represented His crown of thorns. The three stigmas represented the three nails and the five anthers below them His five wounds.

Remarkably, there are more than 500 species of passion flower, many of which we are lucky enough to be able to grow in our British Isles, despite their being native to the tropics of South America. I love to see this unexpected touch of the exotic among my cottage garden flowers, especially when I discover that the vine tendrils bearing the flowers have climbed along the stem of an English rose or are entwined with a wild clematis.

Research shows that in its native surroundings, the passion flower's unique structure requires special pollinators, most notably large bees, hummingbirds or bats. Imagine the beauty of the scene and being lucky enough to witness such a happening.

This adventure into the Amazon rainforest led me to many discoveries – not least to all the many stunning life forms that inhabit it. I have tried to portray just a few in these embroideries, with their rich colours showing up vividly against the background of the lush rainforest. Some of the life forms seem straight from the land of fantasy. I chose to add labradorite, a crystal known for its magical qualities, for this reason.

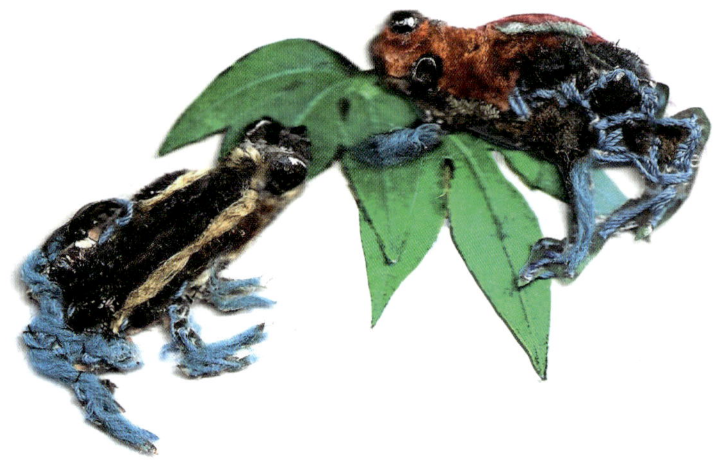

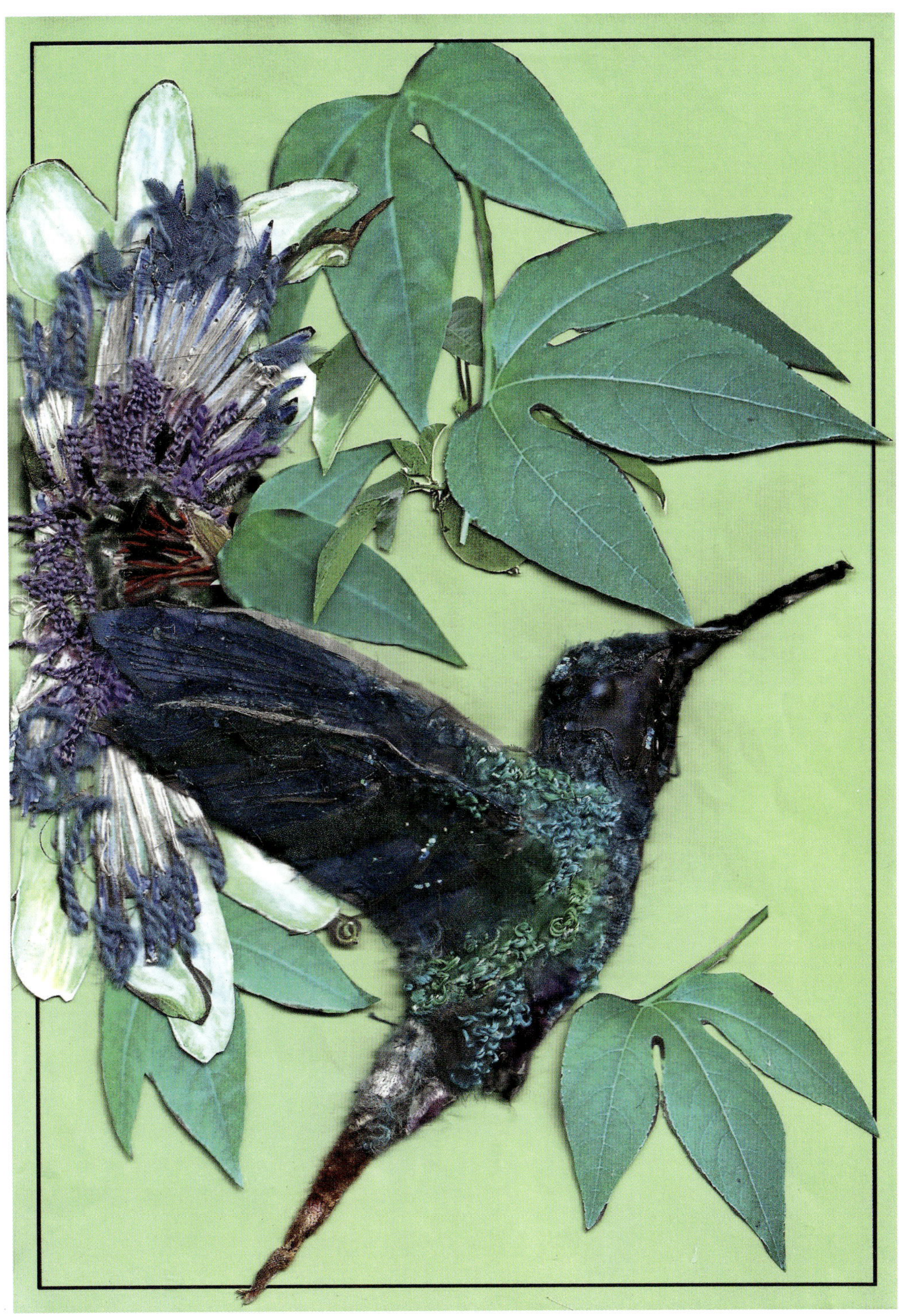

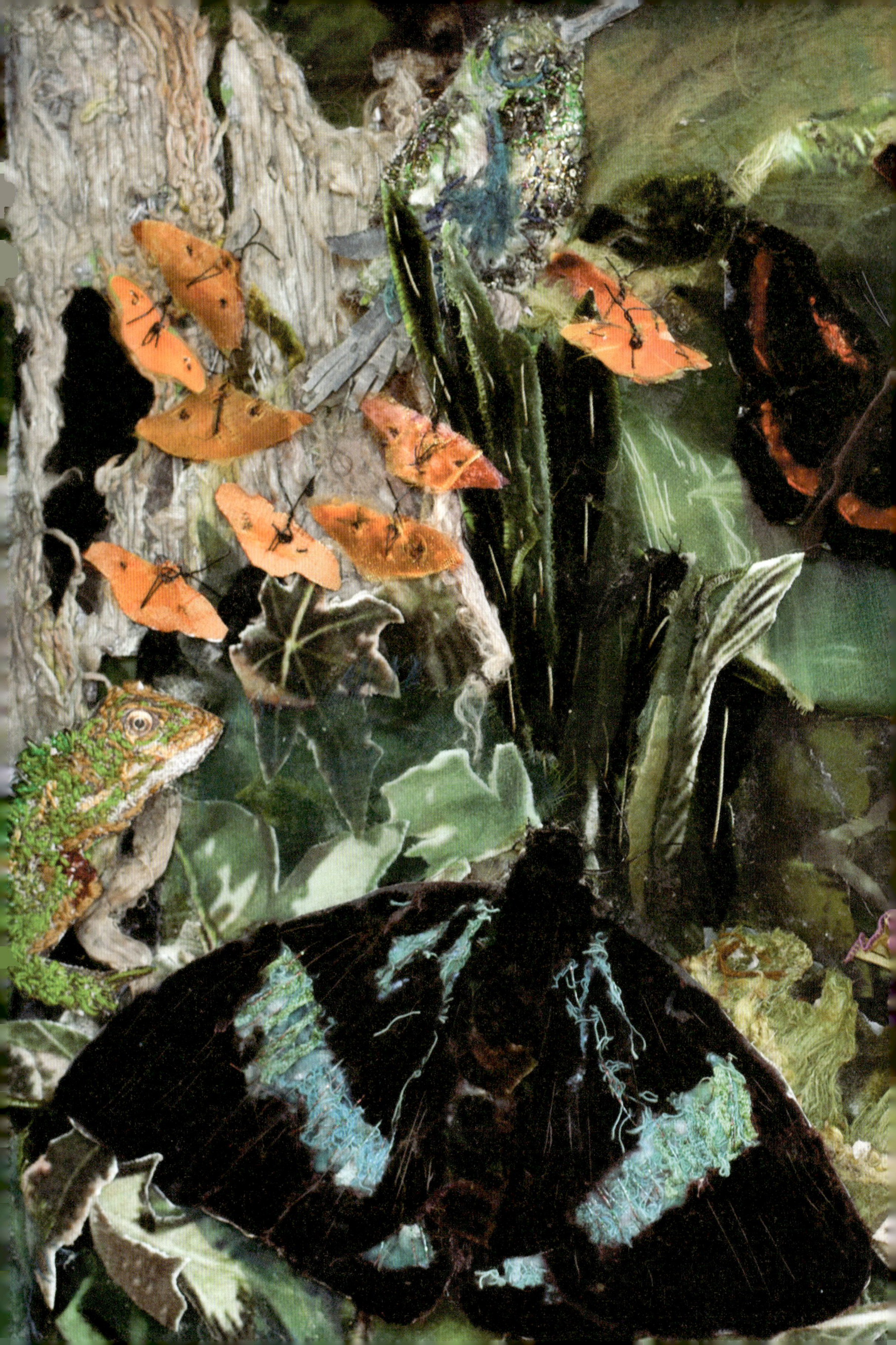

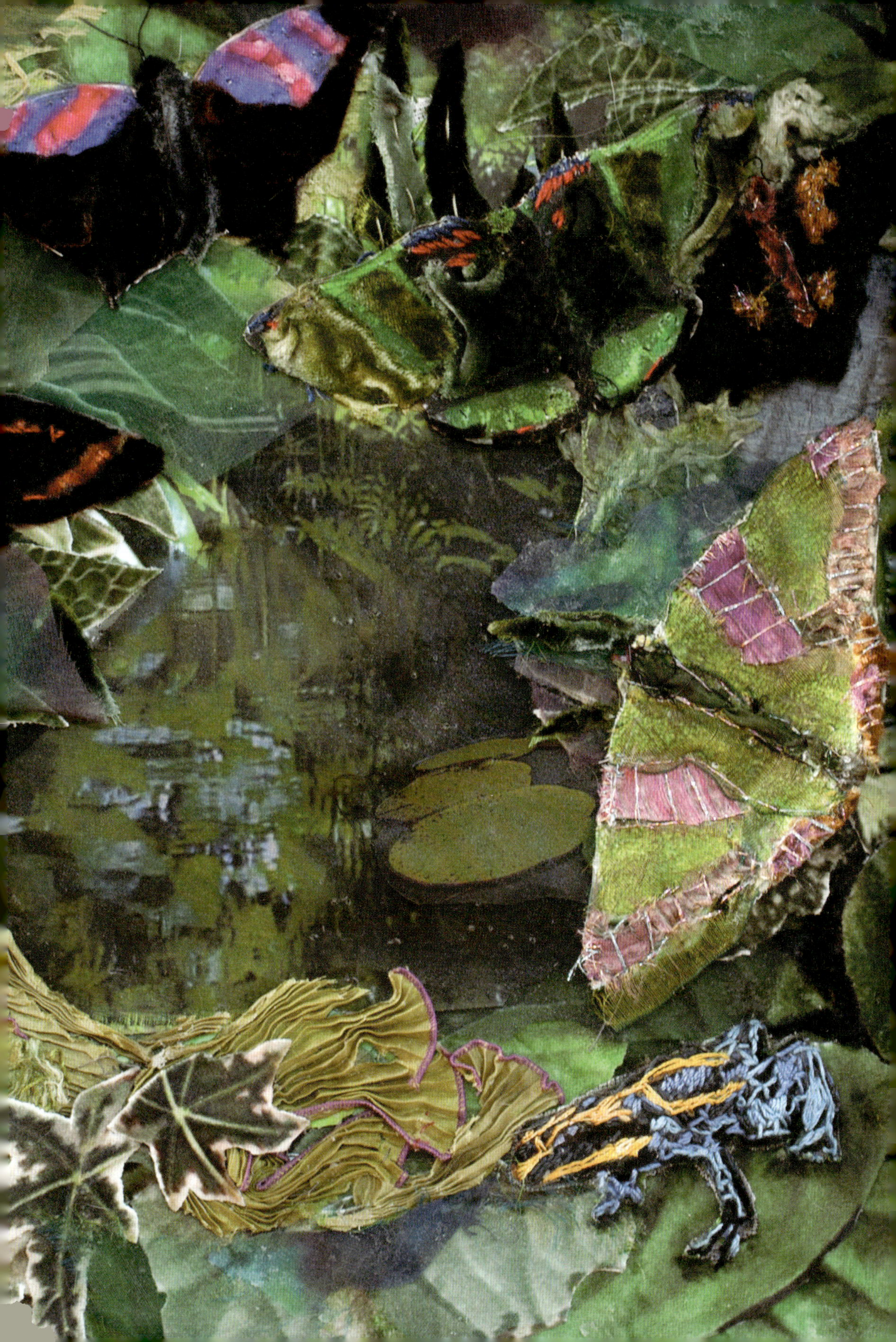

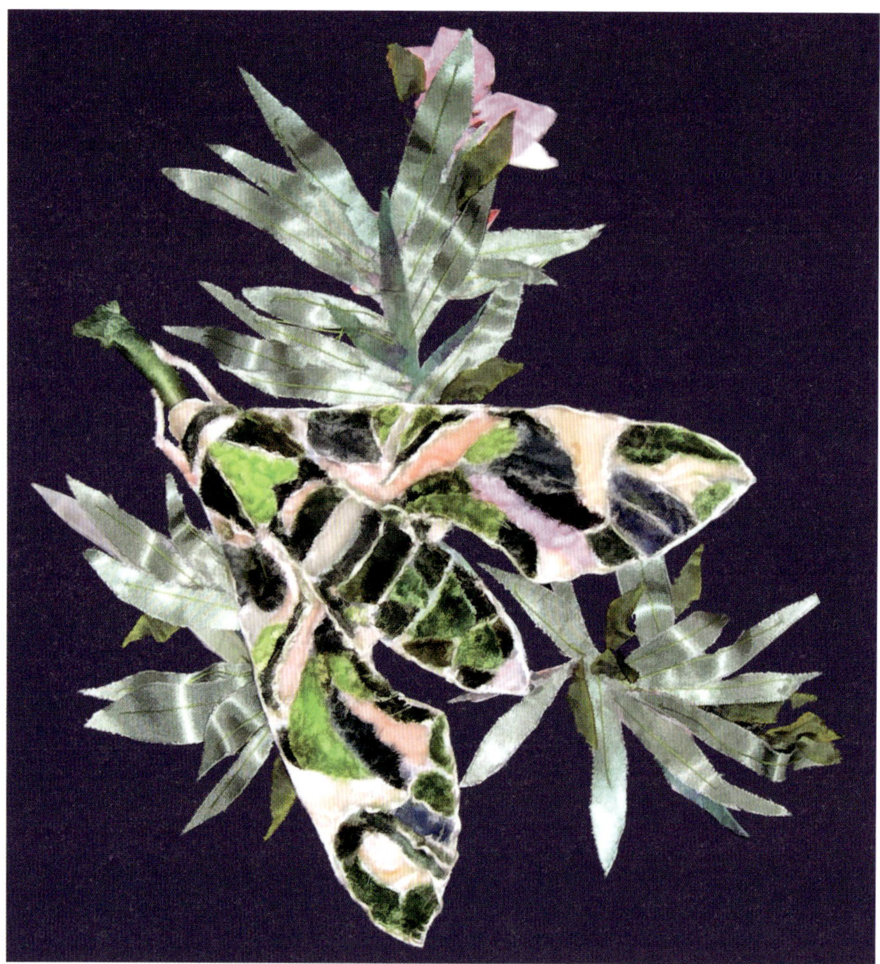

Another beauty capable of acting as a pollinator to the passion flower is the hawk moth, with its long proboscis. In flight and when gathering nectar, hawk moths are often mistaken for hummingbirds. They beat their wings so rapidly that all that can be seen is a blur, often accompanied by a humming sound. This rapid beating allows them to hover in the air, move forwards and backwards, and travel at great speeds. They are the fastest-flying moths in the world; just like hummingbirds, they can fly up to 35mph. One such example is the oleander hawk moth, embroidered here, with the striking colouring and patterning that drew me to broider it. It is a magnificent moth with a wingspan of up to 13cm.

The passion flower began to be used widely in the west as a herbal remedy in the second half of the last century, although it has been used for many centuries by the indigenous peoples of South America in their traditional medicines.

It is a well-known sedative in low doses, but during the First World War it was controversially considered strong enough as a nerve sedative to be used to treat shell shock.

Today the passion flower is still used as a dietary supplement for sleep problems as well as pain, heart rhythm problems, menopausal symptoms and ADHD.

The long list of health benefits is due to the multiple nutrient, mineral and vitamin contents of the fruit, which makes it such a gift to the world of medicine, with the added bonus that the fruit is truly delicious to eat.

A very unusual recipe I discovered for a sleep aid tincture uses passion flower and smoky quartz – known for its stress relieving vibrations.

Ingredients

50g of dried passion flower
50g of dried valerian
500ml of vodka

Method

Place smoky quartz in a small glass jar, and in turn place this in a larger bowl filled with the vodka.
Leave overnight under a full moon or for a full day in pure sunlight.
Remove the crystal and add the vodka to the dried herbs.
Leave to infuse for six weeks, then filter.
Take 10 drops in a little water and a good night's sleep is promised.

Autumntime

Autumn abundance – a season of copper and russet and amber glories, with a golden edge to the haze in the late-afternoon air.

I think of glossy chestnut conkers shedding their prickly armour and the smell of roasted sweet chestnuts selling in the market, and of harvest festivals.

But there is always the nostalgia of the summer passing and the golden haze becoming grey mist as the days shorten and the nights draw in.

FALL, LEAVES, FALL; DIE, FLOWERS, AWAY;
LENGTHEN NIGHT AND SHORTEN DAY;
EVERY LEAF SPEAKS BLISS TO ME
FLUTTERING FROM THE AUTUMN TREE.
I SHALL SMILE WHEN WREATHS OF SNOW
BLOSSOM WHERE THE ROSE SHOULD GROW;
I SHALL SING WHEN NIGHT'S DECAY
USHERS IN A DREARIER DAY.

'Fall, Leaves, Fall' – Emily Brontë

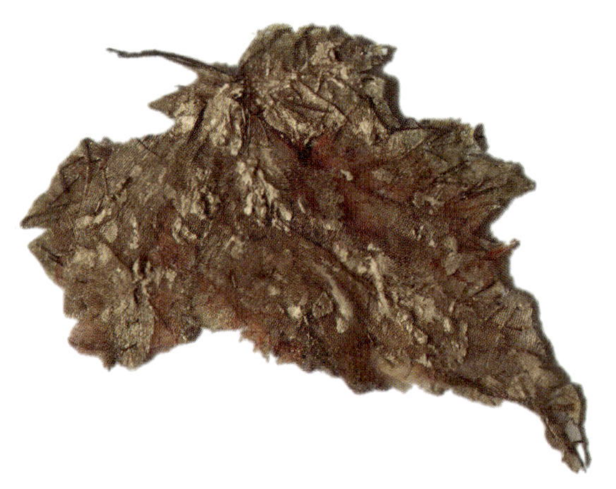

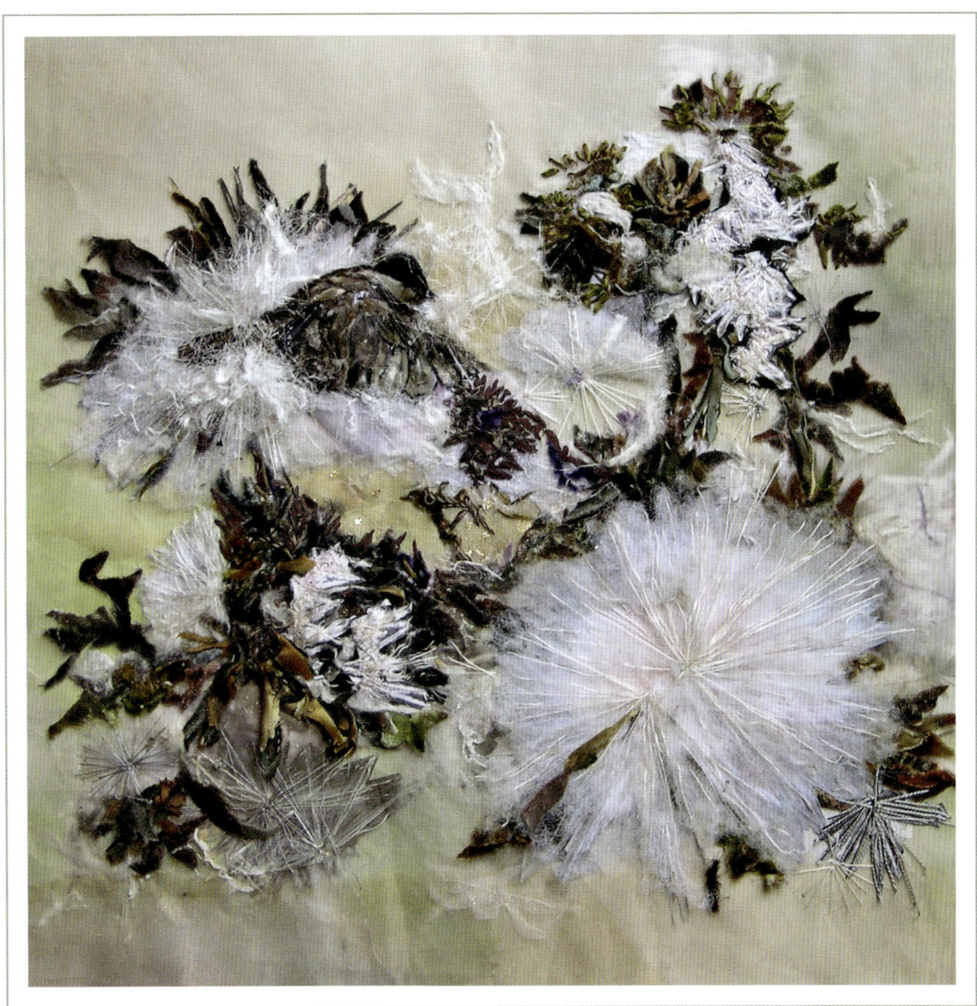

FALLEN LEAVES create the perfect environment for all sorts of different things. I loved the task of collecting different shapes and colours of fallen leaves for the embroidery I had in my mind. Some leaves remained vivid, others were faded and some skeletal, but all were individual and beautiful. It was really absorbing to try to recreate the textures and structures of each leaf, and each leaf definitely dictated its own character to me as I embroidered. Moss agate was the natural choice for the autumn embroideries, linking as it does with the earth and nature.

Rustle through the leaves, mulch them, store root crops such as beets, carrots and parsnips nestled in them to keep through the winter.

By accident I will turn over a leaf in the garden to find a stag beetle, a hibernating moth or a lacewing. The whole world of the curious forms of nature which are lying hidden and sheltered. Bees, moths, butterflies, snails and spiders all use fallen leaves for their winter resting place. The mated queen bumble bee burrows only an inch or two into the earth to hibernate for winter, relying on the natural leaf litter for insulation.

I have placed several 'bug hotels' around the garden for whatever insect would like to use them. Just some logs and broken pots and bark and twigs piled together. I see many beautiful frosted spiders' webs around the 'hotels' but can never be sure who is sleeping inside.

The spiders' webs, however, are an unexpected gift that then led to further embroideries and a renewed respect for the weaving skills of spiders. I discovered many butterflies also have this skill, as they overwinter as chrysalises or cocoons, delicately crafted and disguised as dry leaves, which also proved to be a lovely subject to embroider, using dry leaves myself to do so.

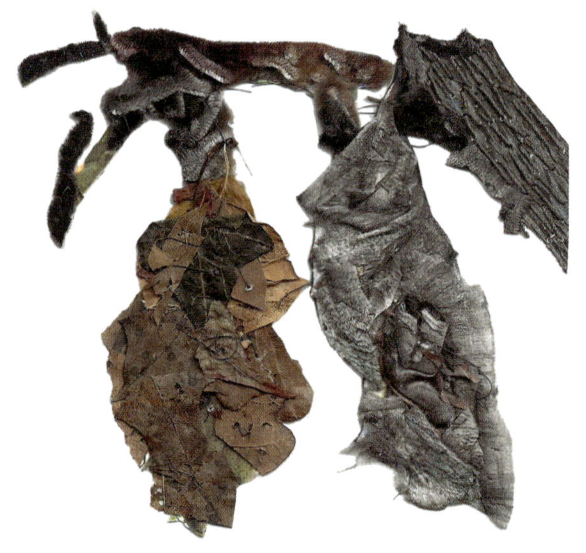

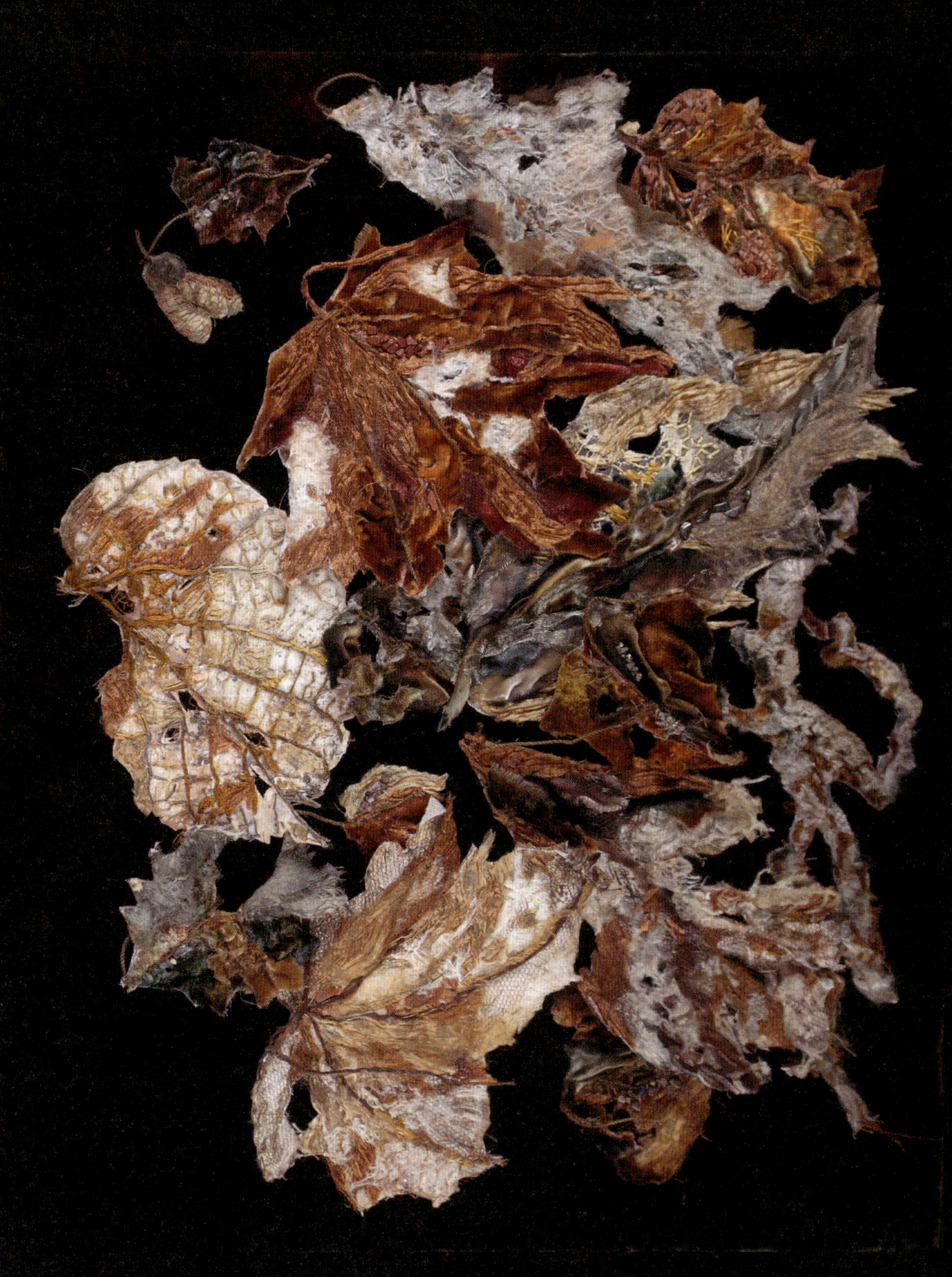

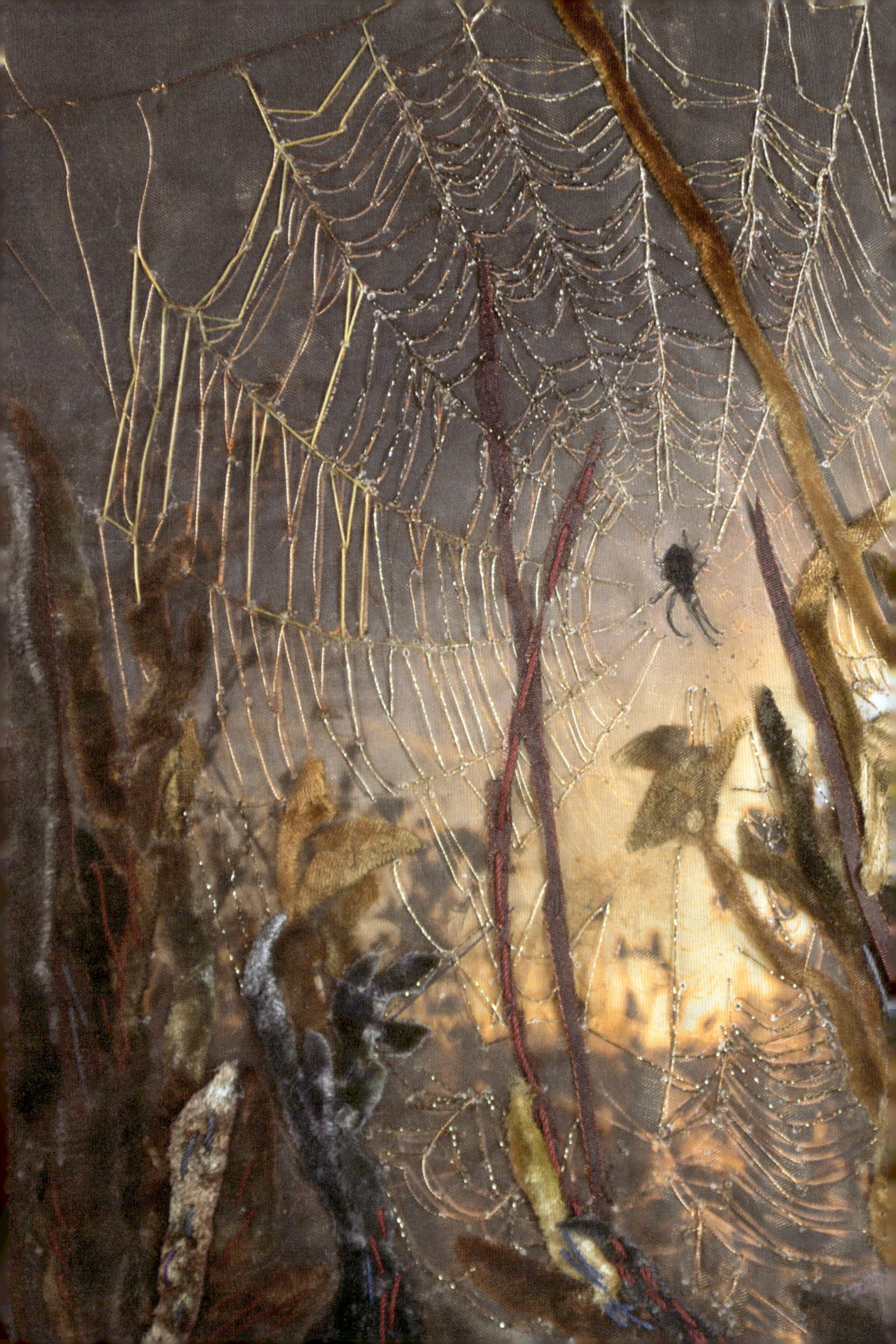

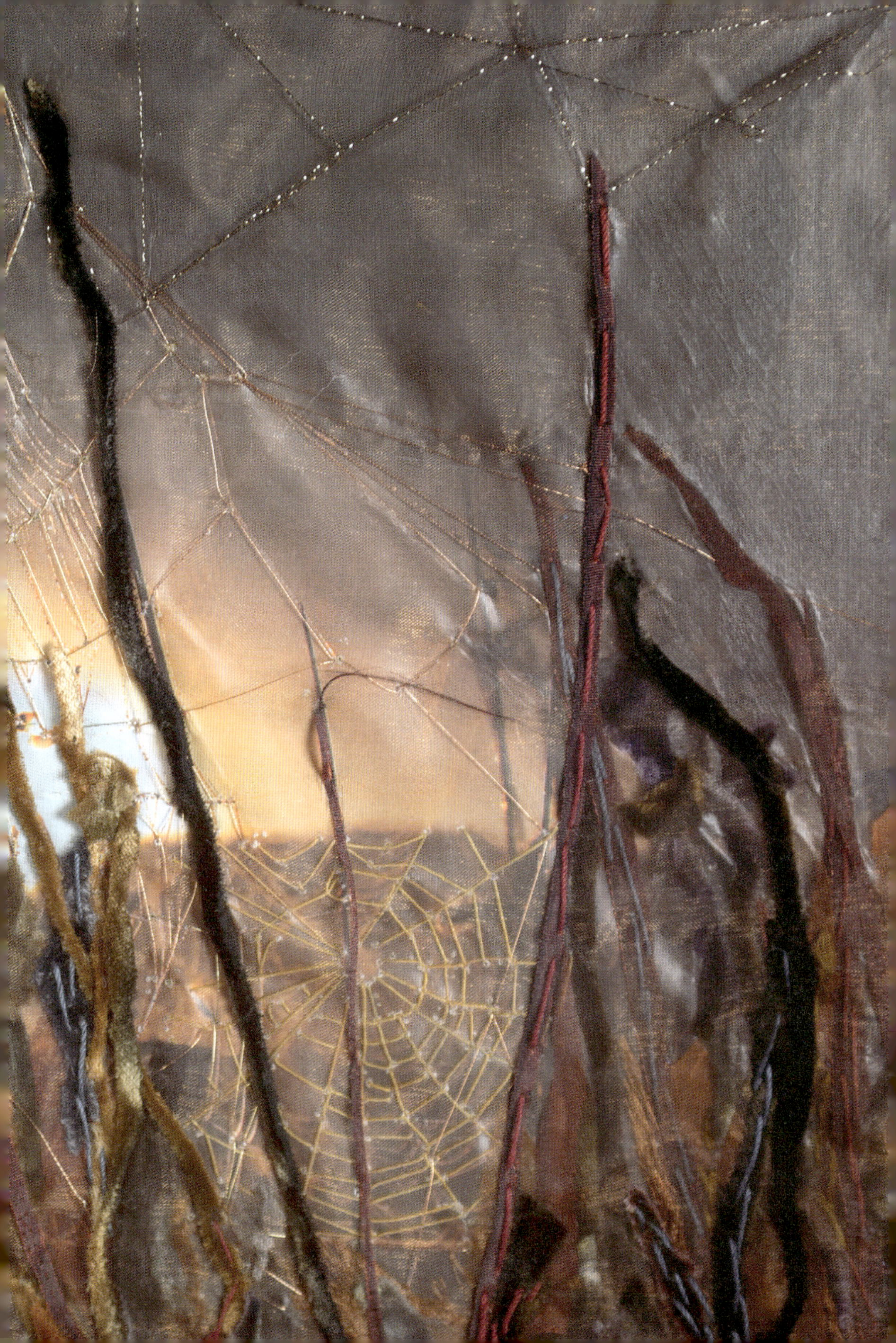

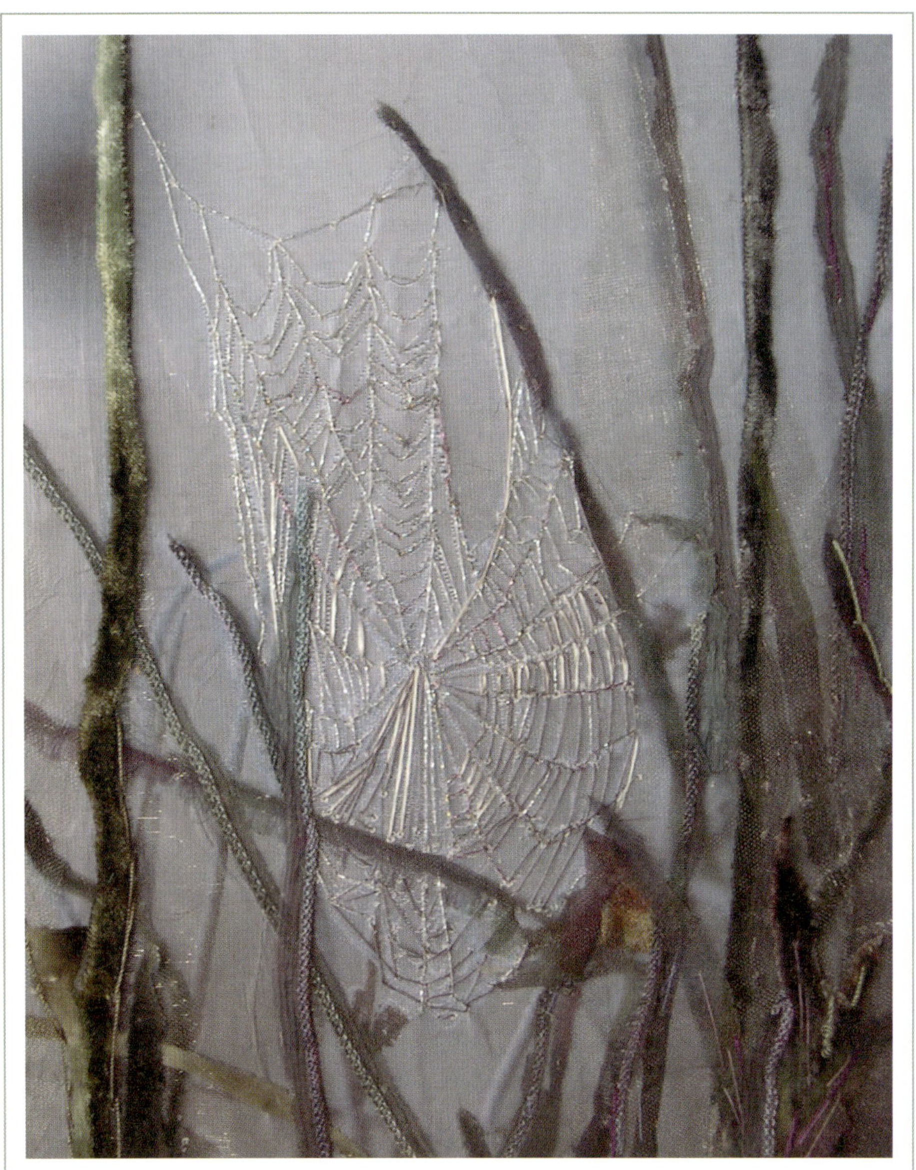

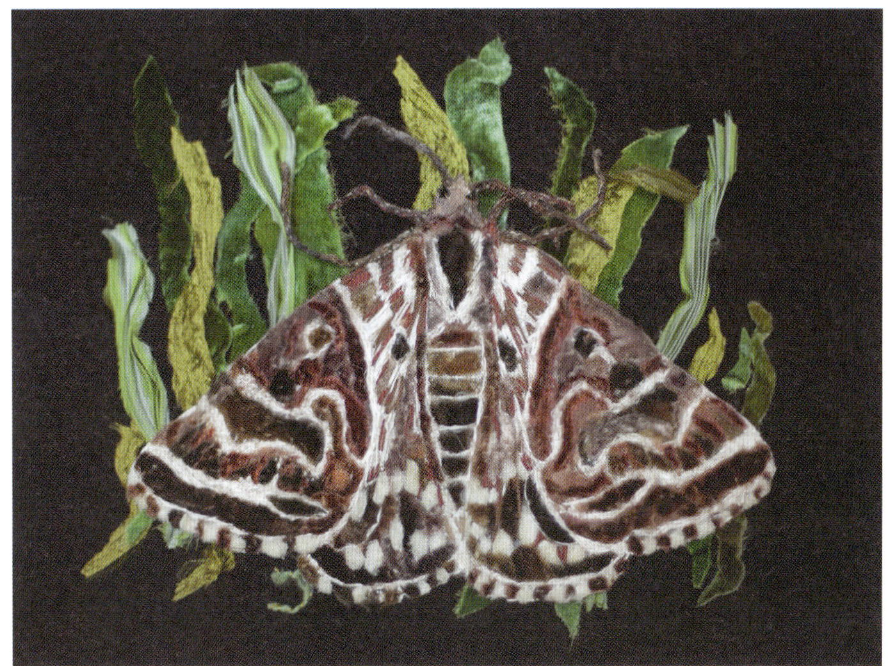

An overwintering moth is the Mother Shipton moth with its perfect autumn colouring. This not only made it a pleasure to embroider because of the rich colours, but it was also the intriguing details of the patterning that really interested me. The moth is named after Old Mother Shipton, the sixteenth-century Yorkshire prophetess, because the outline of a witch's face which Mother Shipton resembled, with its hooked nose and long pointed chin, can be seen on both of its forewings.

Mother Shipton is England's most famous prophetess. Records say that her appearance caused her to become a recluse and she spent most of her days around the cave where she was born, studying the flowers and herbs, and making remedies for the local inhabitants. But she also had another gift: she could foretell the future. Such was her fame that she was even mentioned in Samuel Pepys' Diary. She supposedly foretold the invention of iron ships, horseless carriages, the Great Fire of London and the defeat of the Spanish Armada. After her death she became part of English folklore and legend.

Mother Shipton is the English name for this beautiful moth; it has other common names in different countries as it has a remarkably wide-ranging habitat from Europe to Siberia and the Far East.

I am lucky enough to have many trees in my garden, because every tree, whatever species, has a very powerful presence in the landscape. It is equally important beneath the earth, which led me to the fungi embroideries.

Research suggests that related plants and trees in a wood help each other, with parent trees helping their saplings. The trees are part of a vast interconnecting underground network of organisms, called the mycelium, which allow the nutrients to pass between them and for the seedlings to be nurtured. This brings to my mind all the wonderful magical woods we read about in literature. So I wanted to include in the fungi embroideries the layers of leaf, loam and lichens that are also a part of the tracery of the woodland undergrowth. This abundant detail of allure, with all its strange shapes, colours and structures is often overlooked, but it plays an important part in the life cycle of the woods, and it provided exciting textures to replicate. I used torn and shredded mulberry leaves, mica, twigs and feathers, materials and threads.

Root fungi are the main conduit of this nourishment between trees and plants. The familiar mushroom shape of fungus that we recognise is only the fruiting body, as most of the fungus is actually underground, forming a complex and intricate woven web. This is now known as the Wood Wide Web, which again conjures up in my mind stories of magic.

The impressive fungi are also one of the most important decomposers of dead organic matter. Scarce but biologically essential elements such as nitrogen and phosphorus would otherwise remain trapped in a habitat, and without these elements plants and crops cannot flourish – and neither can we.

Such is the wonder of fungi that there is a fungus known as the honey mushroom which is the largest living organism on the planet, covering over 2,000 acres of the Malheur National Forest in the Blue Mountains of Oregon. It is thought to be around 8,650 years old.

Whilst scientists have classified many of the fungi in nature, it is estimated that there are still vast numbers that remain unclassified, so their potential is as yet unknown and simply waiting for discovery.

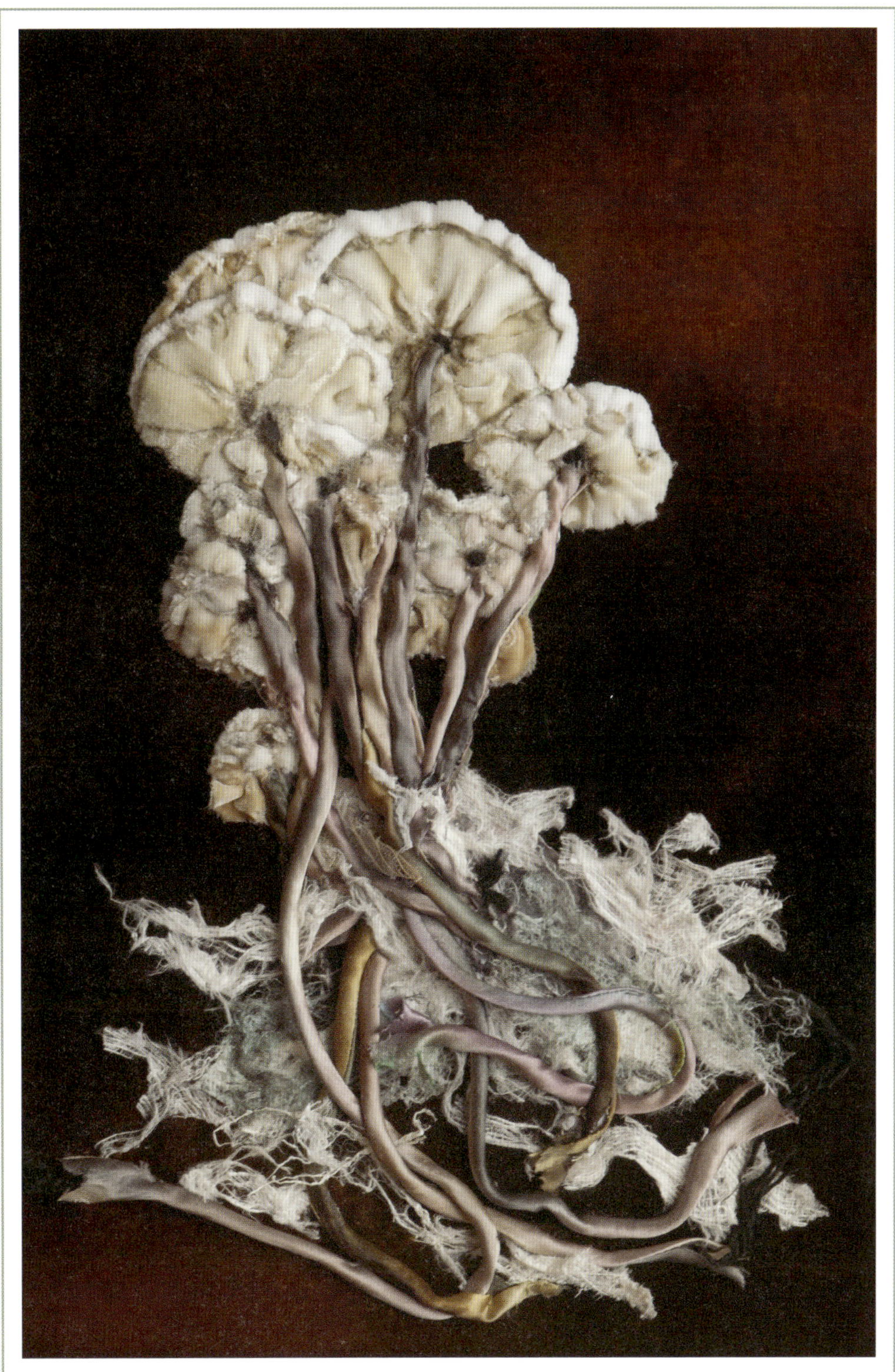

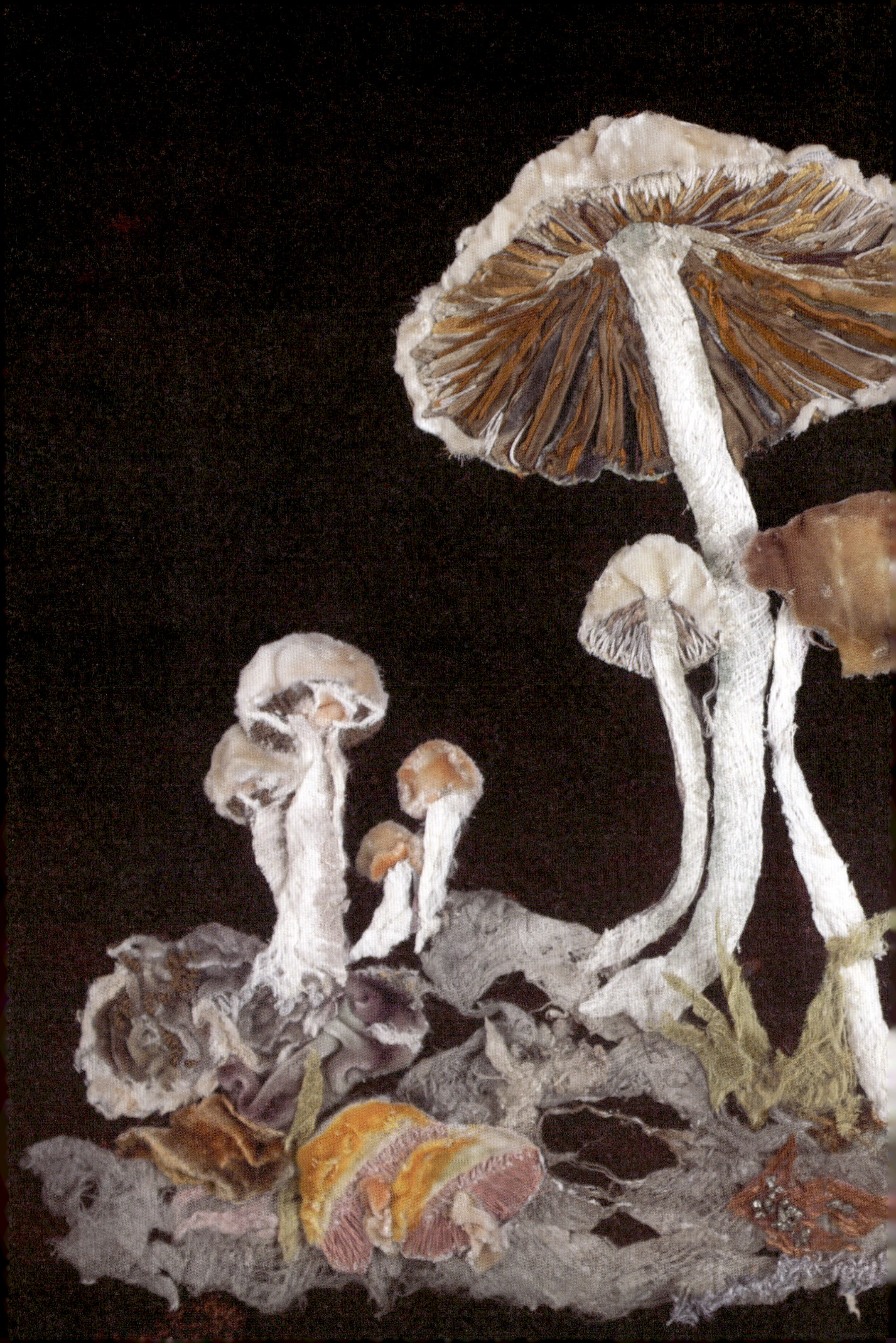

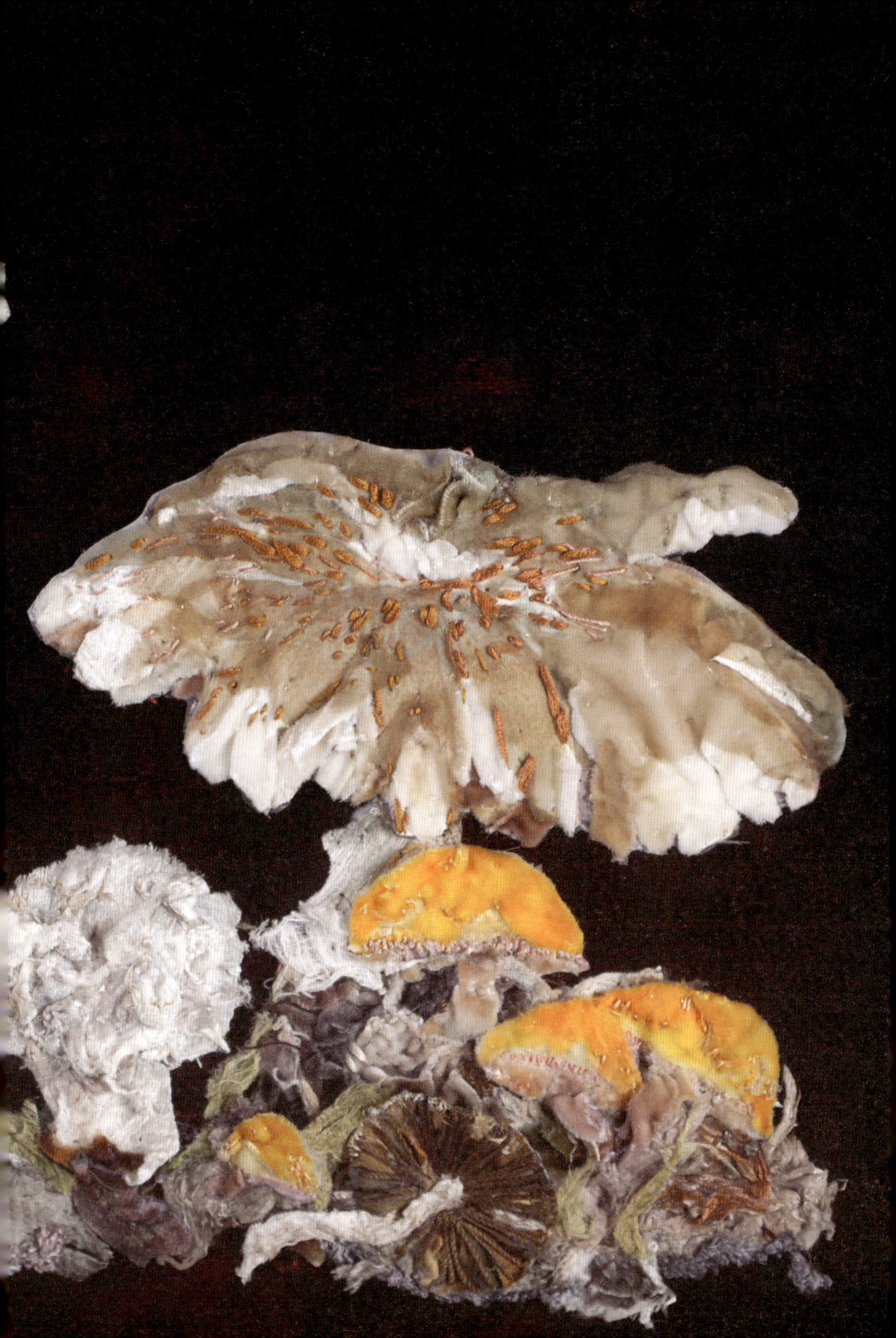

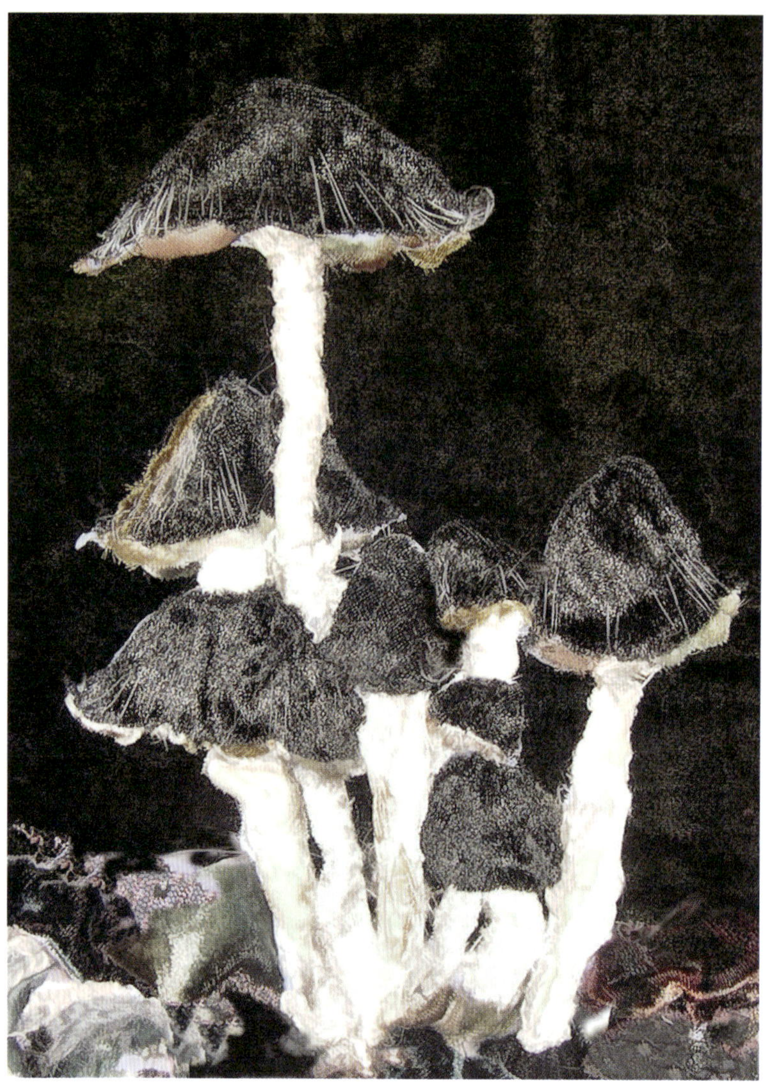

Black Inkcaps, as well as being magic mushrooms used for psychotropic intent, are also useful. The caps dissolve themselves to form a permanent black ink that can be used for artwork.

Method
Remove the caps of a handful of inkcap mushrooms.
Place in a container, add a little boiling water and some cloves.
Leave for a few days or until fully dissolved.

It is always a wonder to me to witness the sudden appearance of mushrooms, toadstools and fairy rings that have materialised overnight. This fascination with fungi and their life forms grew deeper because their textures and shapes and variety were so intriguing to me. I found that bringing them to life required very intricate embroidery – although the final forms appeared deceptively simple, just as the fungus itself does. The background research I did for these embroideries then led to interesting discoveries.

The first discovery was just how long medicinal mushrooms have been used for healing. Ötzi – the 'Iceman' – Europe's oldest known mummy at around 5,300 years old, from the Copper Age, was found with two types of medicinal mushrooms: one strung on cords around his neck and the other in his pouch. The types have been identified as birch polypore, used as a medicine for parasites, and tinder polypore, which enabled him to light fires and carry smouldering embers from one campsite to the next, but also used as an antiviral and as bandages. They were essential provisions for a travelling man.

We know medicinal mushrooms have also been in use for thousands of years in other cultures. They have been a cornerstone of Chinese medicine, and mention of them is found in both ancient Greek and Roman medical books. In modern times they are being used as natural agents in the prevention and treatment of diseases such as cancer, heart and lung disease and diabetes. Unsurprisingly, they are being hailed as powerhouses of healing.

Magic mushrooms, as distinct from medicinal mushrooms, are being investigated as a cure for illnesses of the mind. According to some scientific research, investigations into fractal geometry coupled with the use of magic mushrooms give the hope that work on this research will lead to effective treatment of mental health conditions. Fractals are common visions for people who use psychedelic mushrooms. Fractals are described as never-ending patterns of infinite intricacy and likened to the formula that depicts the never-ending circle of life. Fractals are some of the most beautiful and complex images to be found in nature. Alchemy at its most magical.

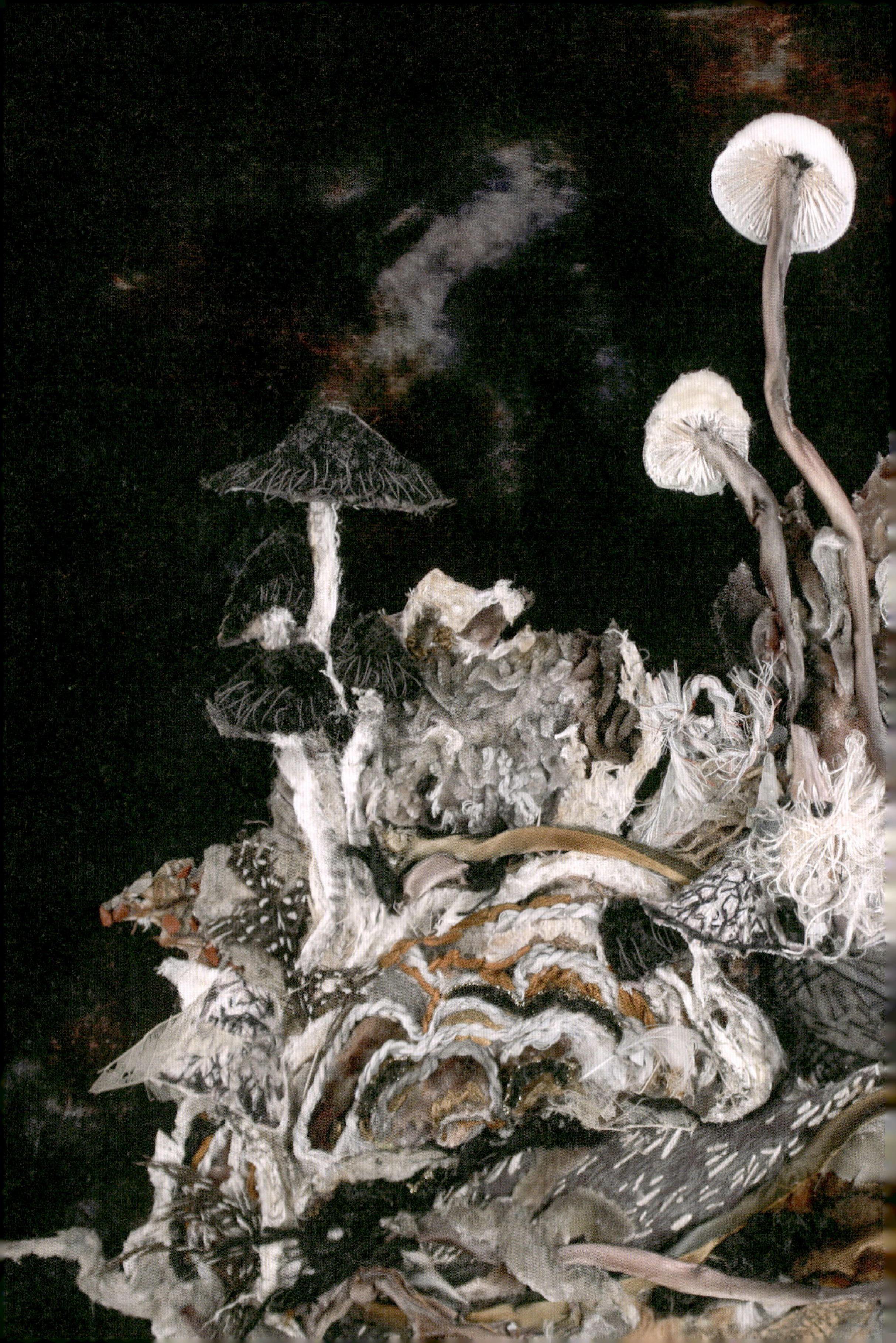

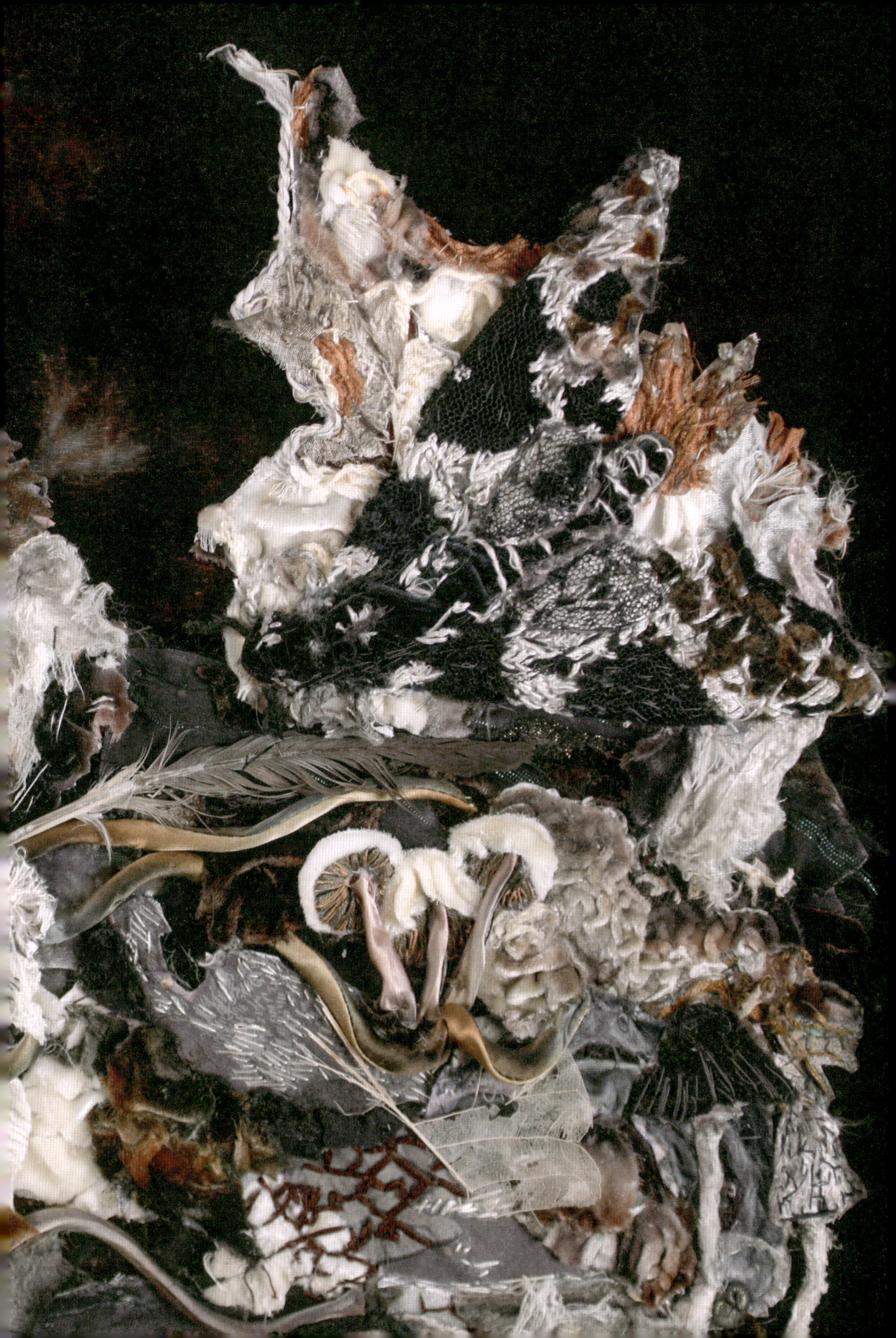

Wintertime

I think of the sight of icicles and feathery hoar frost on trees with ice flowers on the window pane, and then, as winter takes hold, I see a snow-clad world, where the shapes of the landscape reveal themselves as black-and-white architectural sculptures.

The topiary in the garden reminds me of black and white chess pieces on a white onyx chessboard set as sentinels beside the frozen pond. There is an opportunistic heron who always comes to investigate, but he takes heed and flies away.

WINTER is the season when the whole world seems to go to sleep. The weather is cold, the ground is hard, and the plants and trees seem frozen in death whilst the earth rests. But life is still there, hidden out of sight. In the garden I can see the single line of footprints from a solitary fox, and then, further on, beneath the trees, the skitterings from field mice and the larger footprints and claw marks from a badger foraging through the snow and ice.

For the Zuni people of New Mexico, the Winter Solstice signifies the beginning of the year. An ancient Iranian festival calls it the Night of Birth and celebrates the triumph of the sun god as the sun begins its tilt back towards the northern hemisphere.

These winter embroideries were intriguing to create, using only a black-and-white palette and trying to convey the crystalline structure of snow and ice through many depths of crusted stitch, thinking of the crunch of walking on frozen snow. I made them in winter, sitting by the warmth of the fire.

Clear quartz, 'the breath from a white dragon', seemed a lovely crystal to use in this work. The blackbird embroidery also has labradorite added to it because the blackbird is such a magical bird.

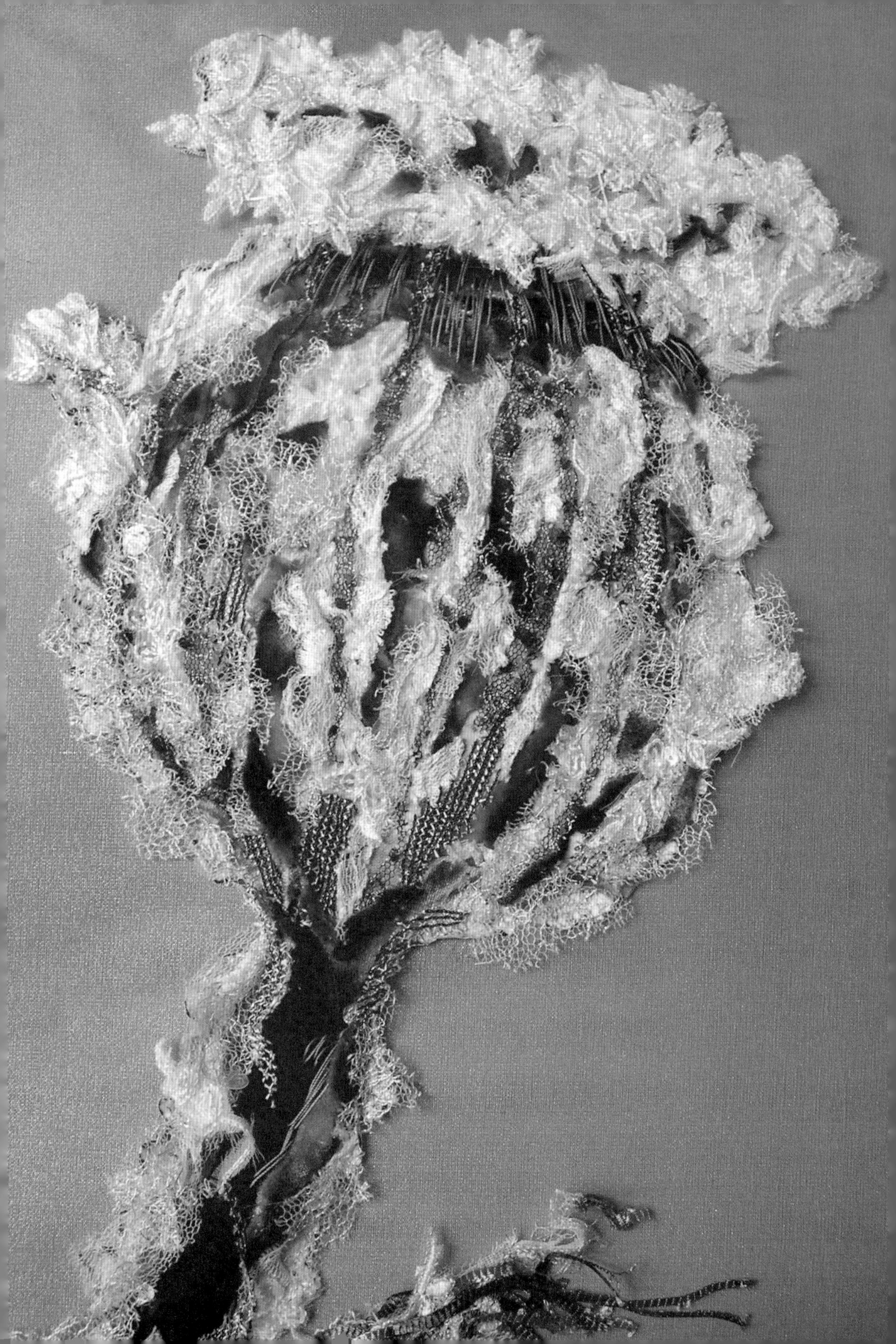

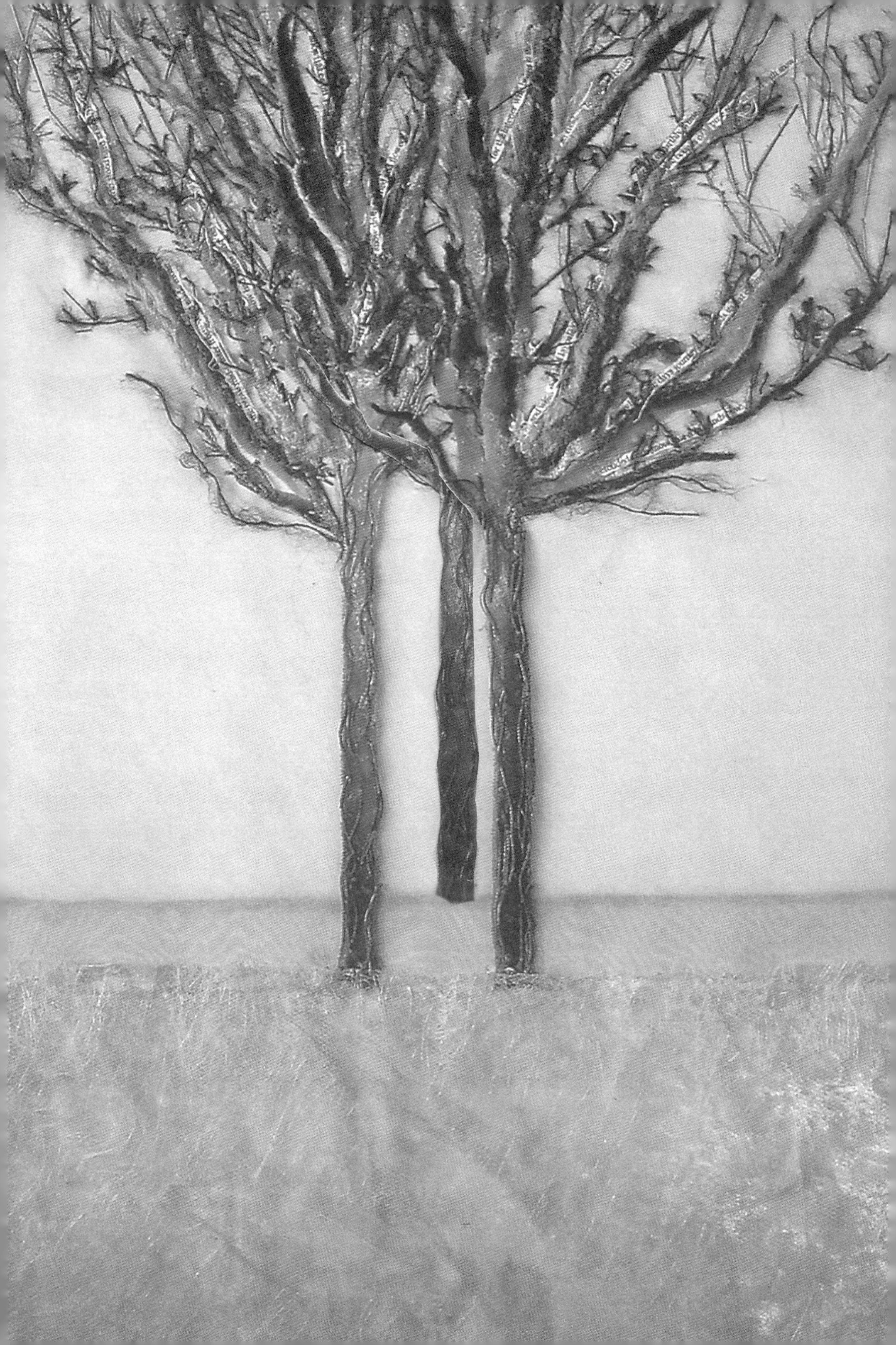

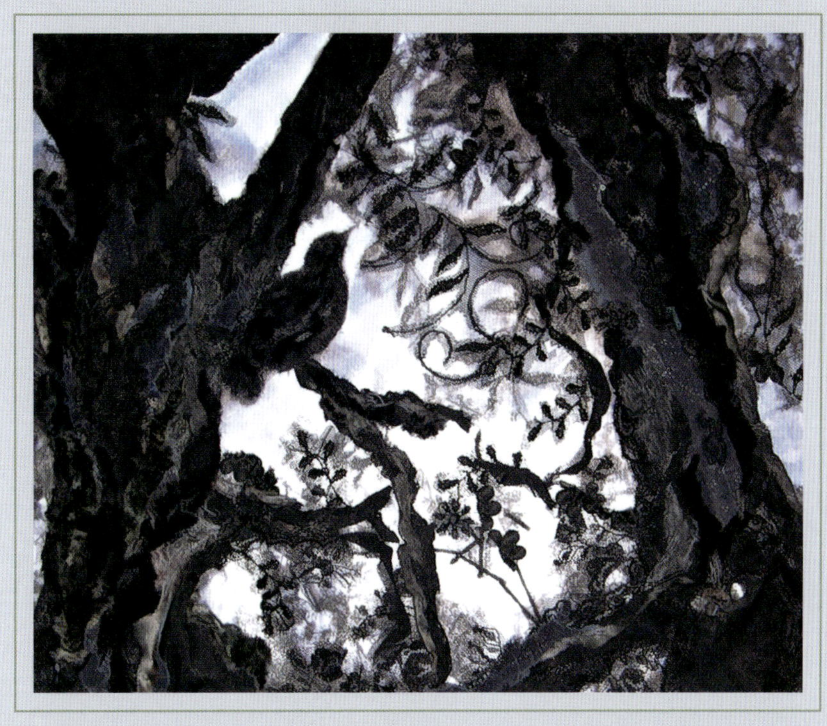

...FOR THE LISTENER, WHO LISTENS IN THE SNOW,
AND, NOTHING HIMSELF, BEHOLDS
NOTHING THAT IS NOT THERE
AND THE NOTHING THAT IS.

'The Snow Man', Wallace Stevens

The delicate and graceful snowdrop is another flower which has collected an array of names.

The snowdrop has been called the Candlemas Bell as it was said to first bloom on Candlemas Day. But in the contest between paganism and Christianity, the festival of Imbolc, celebrating the day that is midpoint between the Winter Solstice and Spring Equinox, claimed that it first flowered on its day of celebration which was the day before Candlemas Day. In competition, each festival involved the lighting of flaming torches and candles: Imbolc to celebrate the increasing strength of the sun bringing warmth and light; Candlemas as the festival day of the candles when all the candles to be lit throughout the year had a blessing said over them. When I designed the snowdrop embroidery, overleaf on the right, I chose to embroider a few of the many different varieties of snowdrops and set them against a backdrop reflecting the glow of those lights.

Candlemas Day is also the day the church celebrated the Virgin Mary's purification, so another name given to snowdrops is Mary's Tapers, combining the meanings of the two Christian feast days and, thanks to their pure white petals, honouring her purity.

The name Mary's Tapers was the thought behind the snowdrop embroidery, overleaf on the left, using the simple white of the flower to contrast with the dark blue background and linking the idea of the tapers lighting the darkness.

There are also other names. In certain parts of Switzerland the snowdrop is called the blackbird flower – it is said that with its appearance, the blackbird begins to sing, a very welcome and beautiful sound. The snowdrop has also been given the name snow piercer, due to the special leaf at the top of the stem that allows it to push through layers of snow.

For such a gentle but brave little flower, it provokes huge reactions. Battles have been fought over the ownership of a single bulb and whole lives dedicated to creating a new variety. To date, the highest price paid for just one bulb is £1,850.

I plant these lovely little flowers every year beneath the silver birch trees, because to see drifts of snowdrops is simply an enchantment.

There is a long history of the snowdrop being used for medicinal purposes – its healing properties were even mentioned by Homer. There are many folklore recipes using the snowdrop for skincare in different formats. But, significantly, the flowers used to be thought of as a cure for headaches and as painkillers.

In the 1950s, a Bulgarian pharmacologist noticed local villagers rubbing the plant on their foreheads to ease pain and decided to investigate further. This work led to the isolation of an alkaloid extract of the snowdrop called galantamine that helped inhibit nerve messengers.

This discovery has now led to the creation of important drugs which are being used in the treatment of Alzheimer's disease and malaria. The compound galantamine is claimed to be a memory improvement supplement and a remedy for traumatic brain injuries and injuries to the nervous system. The snowdrop plant also contains a compound called lectin and this is currently being studied for its treatment effects on and benefits against HIV.

As always, I remain amazed at the healing gifts these plants contain.

The white flower that resembles snow has always been regarded as one of the most significant harbingers of spring and returning life and it is revered in many European countries, being seen as a sign of hope and regeneration and resurrection. It is a very much loved flower.

For these reasons, the snowdrop has become iconic as a beautiful symbol of both the ending of the seasons and the beginning of the new seasons to come, taking us from winter to spring and always bringing joy as it takes us from one year to the next.

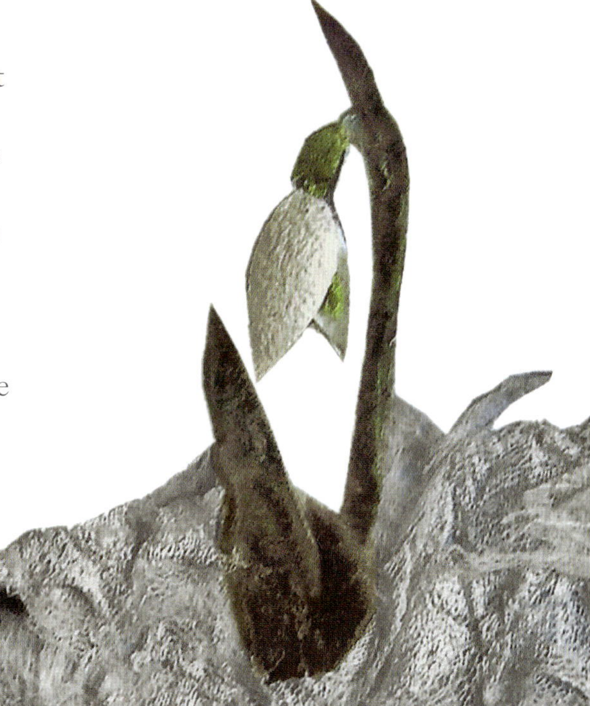

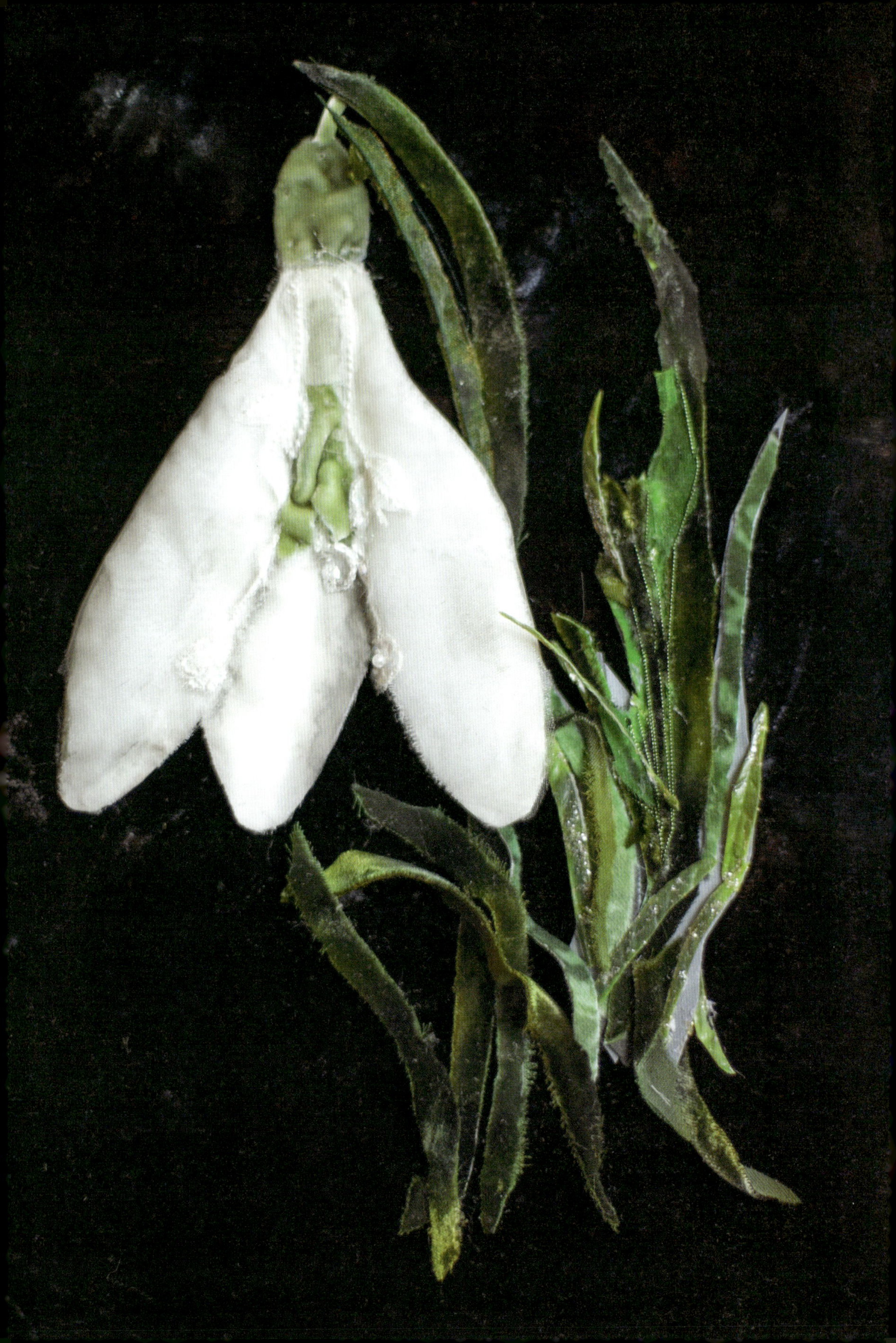

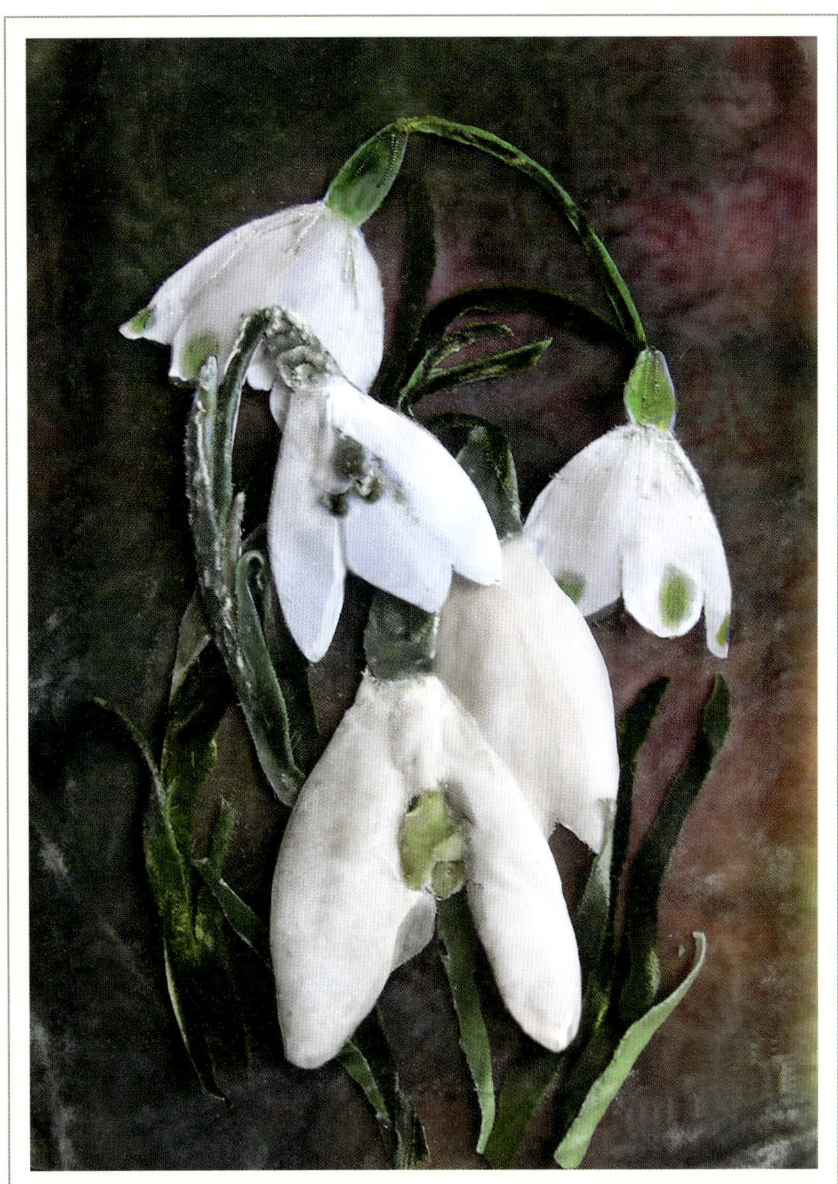

IF A MAN COULD PASS
THROUGH PARADISE IN A
DREAM, AND HAVE A FLOWER
PRESENTED TO HIM AS
A PLEDGE THAT HIS SOUL
HAD REALLY BEEN THERE,
AND IF HE FOUND THAT
FLOWER IN HIS HAND WHEN
HE AWOKE –
AY! AND WHAT THEN?

Samuel Taylor Coleridge

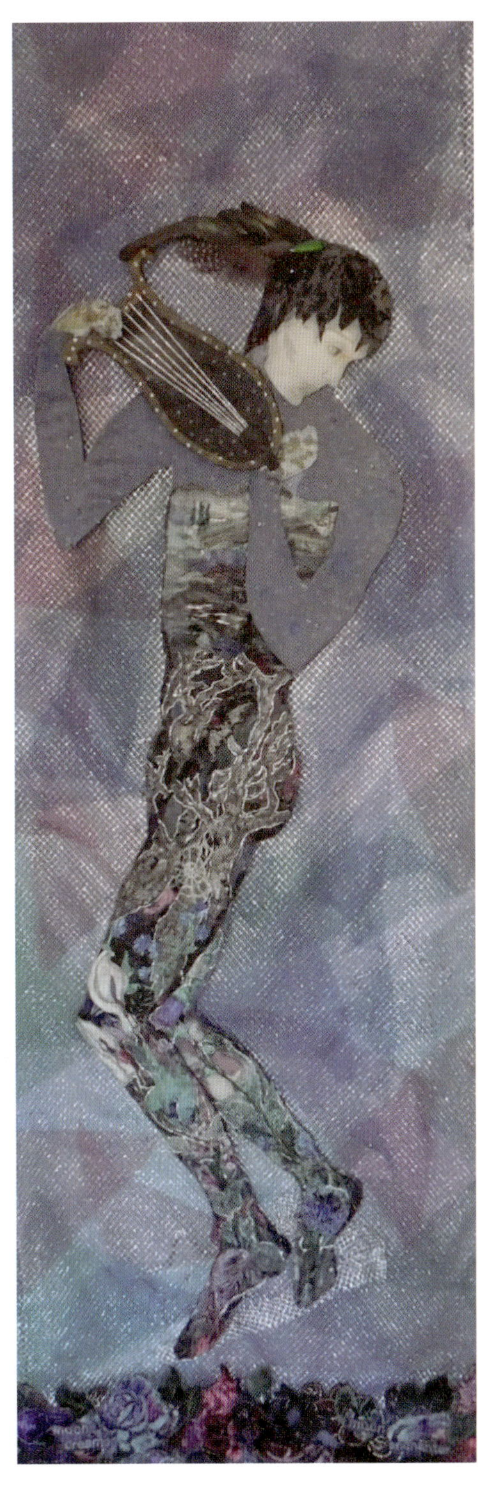

CRYSTALS

IN A CRYSTAL WE HAVE CLEAR EVIDENCE OF THE EXISTENCE OF A FORMATIVE LIFE PRINCIPLE, AND THOUGH WE CANNOT UNDERSTAND THE LIFE OF A CRYSTAL, IT IS NONETHELESS A LIVING BEING.

Nikola Tesla

THE HEALING POWER of nature continues in its minerals. Crystals are not only very beautiful in their infinite variety of colours and shapes and forms, growing deep underground, but for many centuries they have been venerated and used in spiritual rituals. They were prized for their unique energetic qualities and in many religious traditions it was thought that they were descended from the heavens because of the belief in their healing properties.

Crystal caves often appear in tales of magic and mystery as places of healing and infinite marvel. Looking at photographs of the crystal caves found in Mexico, this can be easily understood, as the caves are stunning in their power and beauty.

Today crystals are still very much an important part of our earth, being used not only for healing and energy work, but also for many technical purposes. I have them in my home, placed not only for their energies, but also simply because they are so exquisite to look at, unique in their intricate formation and structure.

Amethyst

Amethyst, which I used in the fritillaria embroideries, is valued as a protective crystal promoting tranquillity and calm, and is often placed in the home and garden for this reason. This lovely crystal, as we know it, is believed to have strong healing and cleansing powers and to enhance spiritual awareness, so I find it empowering that in past centuries it was much used for this purpose.

In the spiritual world, an amethyst crystal provided a connection to the divine.

To the Hebrews, it was Ahlamah, the ninth stone in the breastplate of the High Priest.

To the Egyptians, it was Hemag, listed in the Book of the Dead to be carved into heart-shaped amulets for burial with the dead.

Beads of amethyst have been found in Anglo-Saxon graves in England, suggesting that the people buried with the beads would have a use for them in the afterlife.

From a more worldly point of view, amethyst was thought to prevent intoxication. Ancient Greeks and Romans studded their goblets with amethyst in the belief that wine drunk from an amethyst goblet was powerless to intoxicate. They also believed that an amethyst stone worn in the navel had a sobering effect.

Another use of amethyst was for protection against witchcraft and black magic.

Selenite

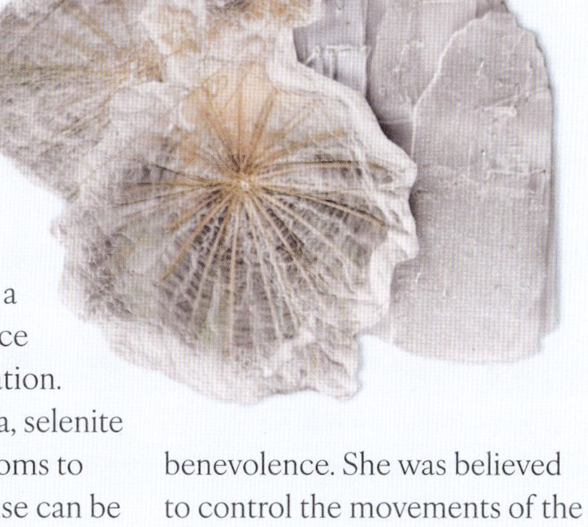

The crystal I used in the noonflower embroideries is selenite, which has clearing and cleansing properties and brings clarity of mind. Selenite is a calm stone that instils peace and is excellent for meditation.

In ancient Mesopotamia, selenite was placed outside sickrooms to keep evil spirits away. Its use can be found in the Bīt Mēseri, which is an ancient Mesopotamian ritual text written on four tablets detailing the exact usage involved. This crystal is named after Selene, the Greek goddess of the moon, who embodied kindness, goodness and benevolence. She was believed to control the movements of the moon as she traversed the night sky in her chariot pulled by snowy white horses. Her radiance shed silvery light upon the earth.

The lapidary of gemstones produced by Alfonso The Learned (Alfonso X), a thirteenth-century king of Castile, echoes her myth in its findings, as it states that selenite is influenced by the waxing and waning of the moon.

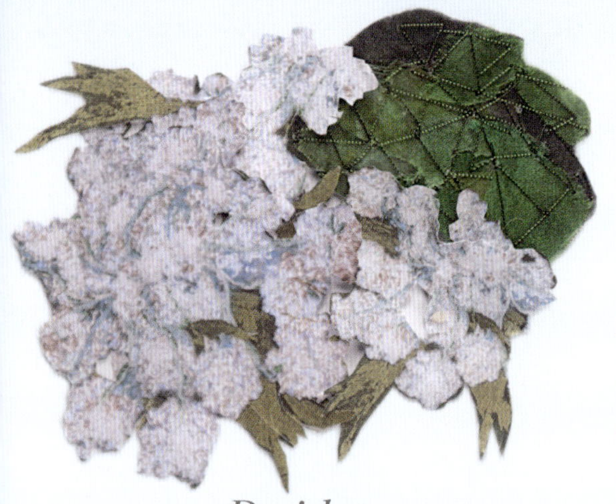

Peridot

The pratice of embedding crystals into hand embroidery is many centuries old.

The crystal used in the cow parsley embroideries is peridot. Peridot's healing properties are used to increase mental focus and perseverance. It is also used for protection against negative energy. It is known as a stone of light.

Ancient Egyptians called the peridot 'the gem of the sun'. Peridot was reputed to be a favourite gem of Cleopatra and Tutankhamun, both of whom wore the stone not just for its beauty but also because it was believed to ward off evil spirits.

Remarkably, the ancient Egyptians' belief about the origins of peridot – that it fell from the sky – has been borne out, not only by its being found in meteorites, but also by NASA's *Stardust* spacecraft returning to earth from outer space with a collection of comet particle samples. Among the samples was found gem-quality peridot.

Ruby

The crystal incorporated into the oriental poppy embroidery is ruby. The ruby promotes love, confidence, loyalty and courage.

Ruby has a host of legends associated with it. Generations in India believed that rubies enabled their owners to live in peace with their enemies. Conversely, in Burma, warriors possessed rubies to make them invincible in battle, inserting the rubies into their flesh to make them part of their bodies.

In the ancient language of Sanskrit, it was called *ratnaraj* (king of precious stones), and Hindus believed that those who offered rubies to the god Krishna would be granted rebirth as emperors.

The Chinese emperor Kublai Khan was said to have offered an entire city in exchange for a single ruby.

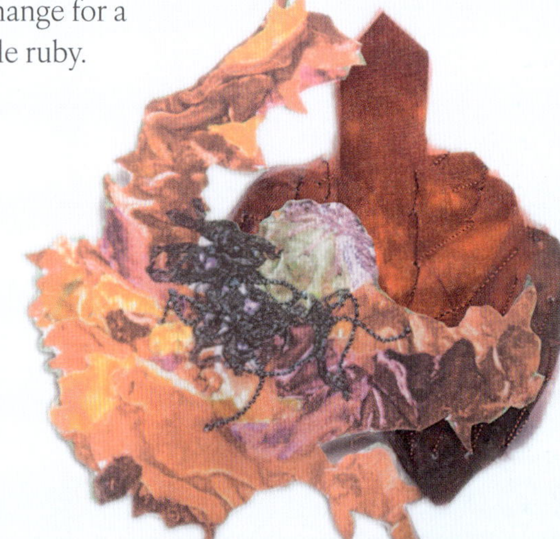

Labradorite

The crystal associated with the passion flower is labradorite – the stone of magic or the shaman's stone of lights. It is the crystal I hold most dear.

Labradorite is supposed to bring good fortune and clear away negativity, and it is an aid to transformation. The stone has been valued by shamans, healers and diviners through the ages.

Inuit legend tells of a warrior who heard the call of the Lights trapped within the rocks on the coast of Labrador. He struck the rocks with his spear to free the Lights. Many were freed and they then wove their way into the sky to form the magical Northern Lights, but some of the Lights decided to remain in the stone, which was given the name of firestone, or fire rock, until it was discovered in 1770 by Moravian missionaries who named it labradorite.

Another legend says that the Mighty Being hit the iridescent rock with his fist to free the lights in order to travel with them into the sky, and the beautiful, elusive Northern Lights have remained as a bridge to the heavens ever since.

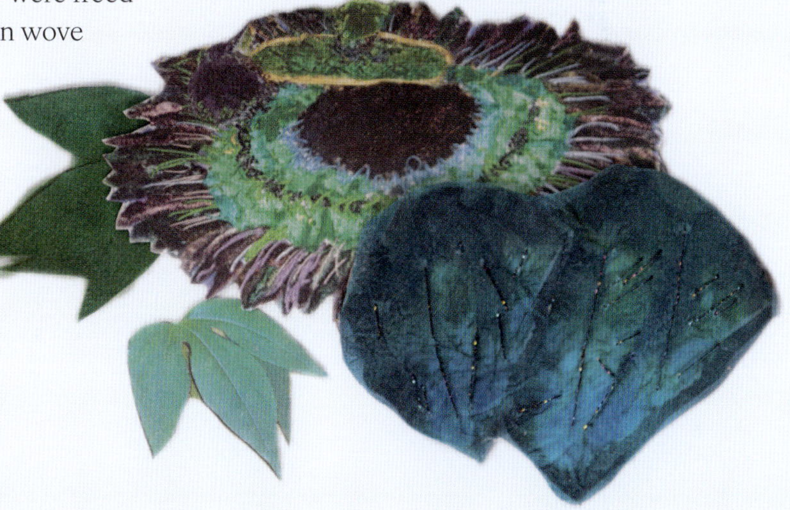

Moss Agate

Moss agate, the crystal of autumn, is said to be a stone of abundance, giving the wearer positive energy and creativity and helping them to see new beginnings in life. I used it in many of the autumn embroideries.

Moss agate is particularly linked to the earth and nature. Many different cultures believed it would help to achieve better harvests and have magical effects on agriculture. Gardeners used to hang one of these stones on a stick or tree to act as a talisman to increase the overall health of plants.

Native Americans believed that moss agate had the power to change the weather, and they would use it in rituals to bring rain.

Pliny the Elder, a Roman historian, quoted the Magi as teaching that storms might be averted by burning agates. And ancient seafarers used agates as protection against fierce storms at sea and to protect from high winds and lightning.

Quartz

The crystal associated with winter is clear quartz. I used it as a wonderful addition to the snow embroideries. The ancient Greeks called quartz *krystallos* (literal meaning coldness drawn together), the word which gave rise to the modern word 'crystal'. Ancient Greek philosophers believed that the transparent stone was permanent ice, so frozen that it never thawed.

People in indigenous South American communities thought that clear quartz skulls held their ancestors' spirits, and the legends surrounding crystal skulls are well known throughout the world.

The ancient Egyptians also believed in this connection of clear quartz to the spirit, trusting that the crystal's energetic power could help the soul progress to the afterlife. In burial rites, they filled cylinders with quartz to balance the Ba and Ka energies of the body to aid in this journey, and clear quartz was also placed on the forehead of the dead to provide safe travel.

In Japanese mythology, the stone was regarded as a symbol of perfection because it was believed to be the breath from a white dragon.

Clear quartz is considered to be a master healer. It is said to take on energies and amplify them, inspiring healing effects. As the stone of light, this clear quartz is also known for its clearing effect, and it has long been used to dispel negative energy as well as aid clarity. It is a brilliant crystal for meditation purposes.

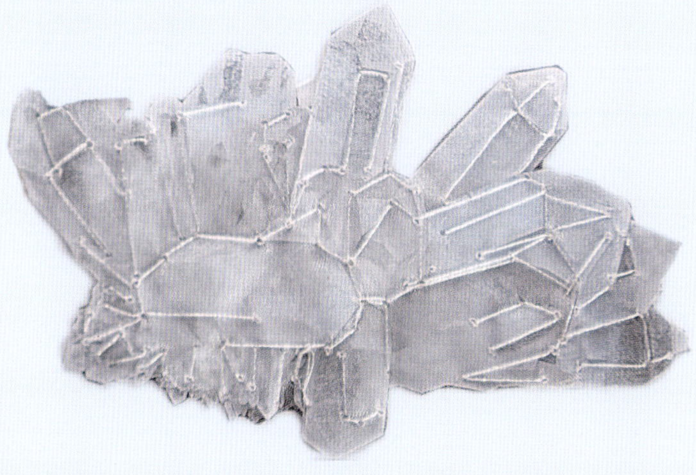

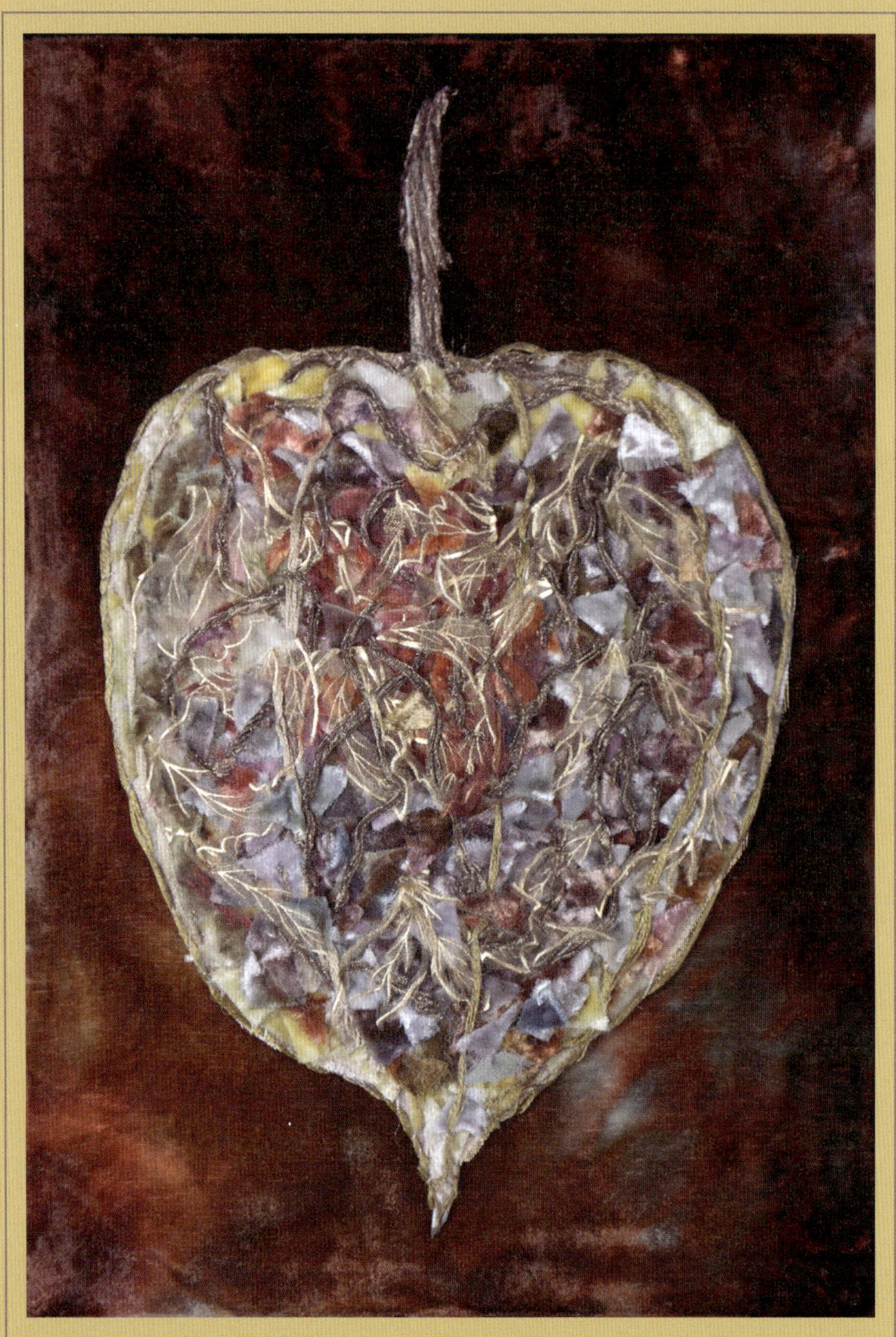

The Art and the Heart of the Needle

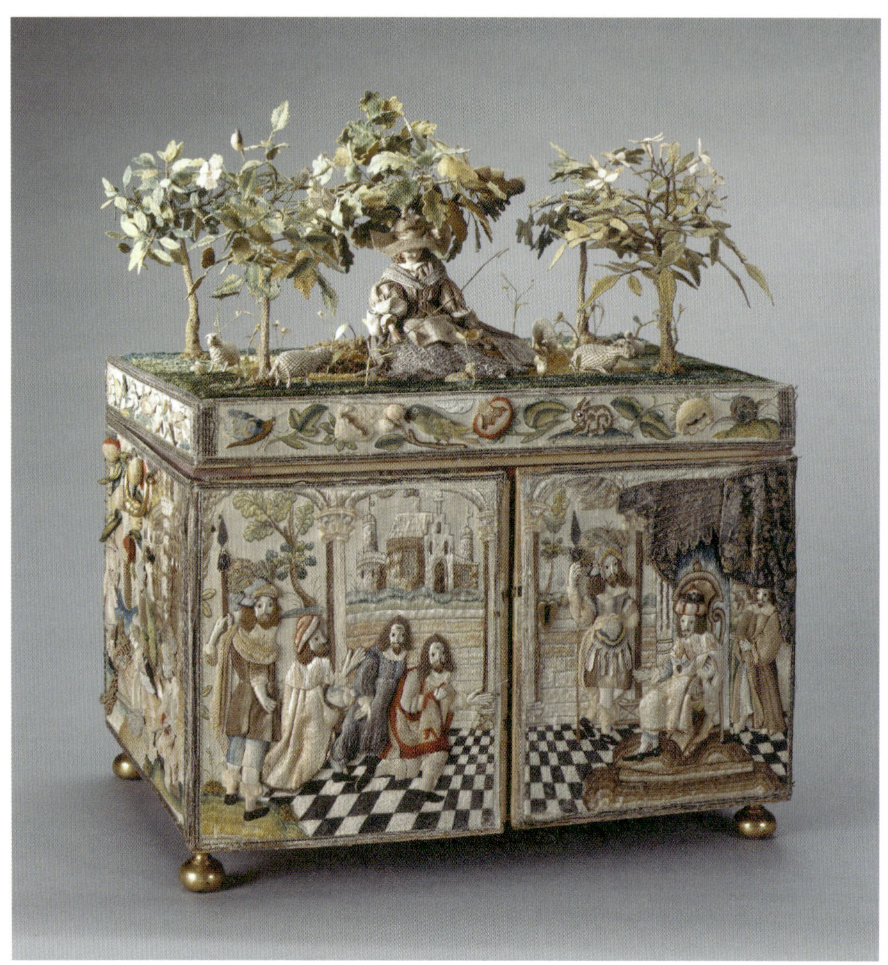

Stumpwork casket *c.* 1660–90

THIS JOURNAL contains past memories and thoughts of the future, and, above all, it records being in the moment through each of the seasons, to receive nature's gifts which speak to the soul. Hand embroidery is a beautiful way to be able to express these things, thinking of both the sky above and the earth below with the wish to show their glory through the eye of the needle.

In this chapter, I have included art from my own collection of embroideries. I thought it could be of interest to share the way that diverse people, from different centuries, cultures and backgrounds have all aspired to honour nature and how their influences have shaped my own work, with the magic of nature the one constant always to be found.

I was first drawn into the world of hand embroidery by the discovery of the little stumpwork casket in the depths of an antique shop, tucked away in a cabinet of treasures. Amongst the flowers, mythological creatures, trees and plants depicted on the casket, there were people to be found, beckoning me to join them. Sometimes it was kings and queens in their castles, other times shepherds and shepherdesses, all set amongst unicorns, lions, parrots and peacocks, butterflies and bees. The figures were all out of proportion and with no apparent context, but all were enchanting. Together, they created a magical world, inviting me to enter and explore the faraway land with them. As a child, I found them to be irresistible. In effect, it was time-travelling in the most exciting way through hand embroidery.

Hand embroidery has been an art form throughout the continents for many centuries, dating back to at least the second millennium BC. Nature has been a consistent theme throughout, the embroidery bearing the message of its beauty and power. Nature in all its abundance was celebrated as a manifestation of the Creator's gift to humankind.

One of the oldest surviving groups of embroideries comes from the tomb of Tutankhamun. Flowers were embroidered on his ceremonial clothing and collars. The flowers have been identified as cornflowers, for their connection to the blue lotus and representing life and fertility, poppies for their connotations of rest and resurrection, and olive leaves, which the ancient Egyptians crowned their pharaohs with in death, representing success.

These were the flowers and leaves that were considered of significant value in ancient Egypt.

The collars were worn on the body during a ceremony that took place before burial, then they were

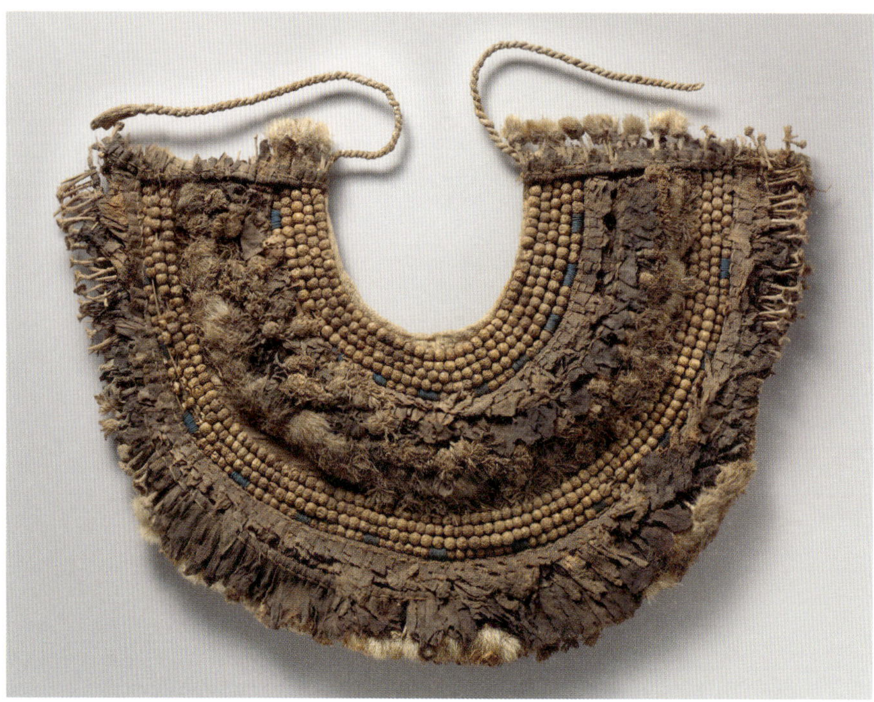

Floral collar from Tutankhamun's embalming cache

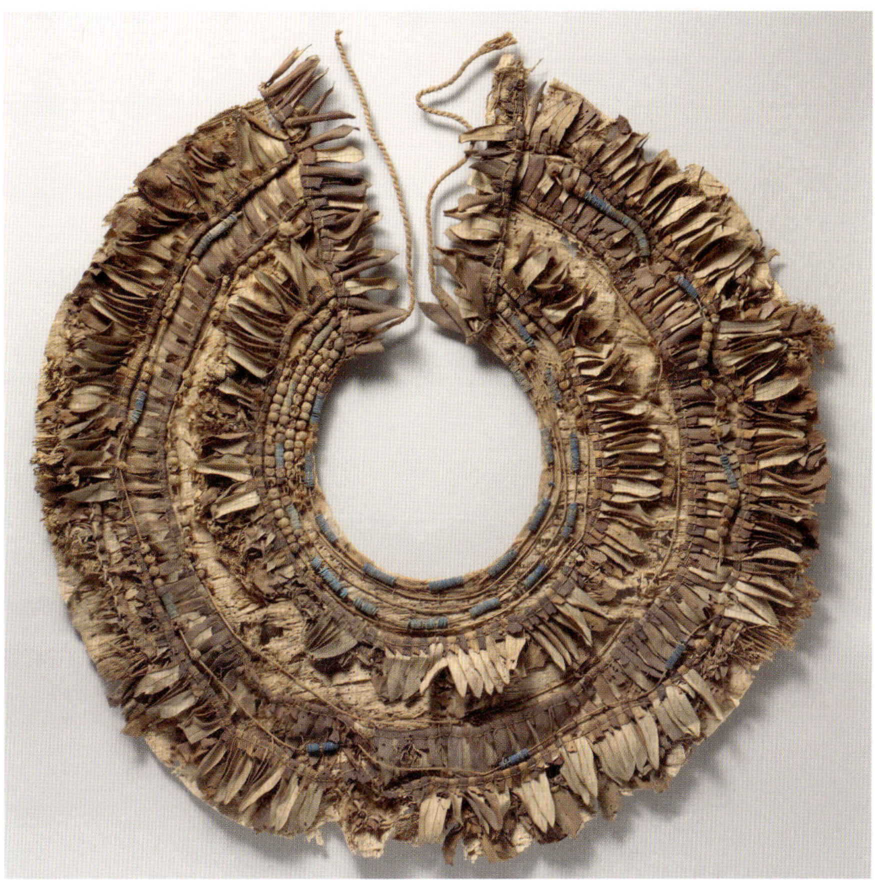

Floral collar from Tutankhamun's embalming cache

removed and placed in pots which were buried apart from the main burial site.

The embroideries for Tutankhamun were made to honour him and give him gorgeous clothing to wear in the afterlife. The richer the broiderers could make the clothing – the more they could embellish it with jewels, gold and embroidered flowers, symbols and emblems of the gods – the more honour they could give him. Although the shapes and colours are now faded, it is possible to imagine what was in the embroiderers' thoughts when they were embroidering the ceremonial garb for their king to wear. The things they knew would be of importance and which their pharaoh would treasure.

Thinking of the burial ceremony, and the riches that were given to him and placed in the burial chamber for his use in the afterlife, the beauty of Tutankhamun's gold death mask made me wish to embroider this death's-head hawk moth in tribute.

Howard Carter's evocative words in his journal on discovering the burial chamber gave me the inspiration.

'I inserted the candle and peered in. At first I could see nothing, the hot air escaping causing the candle to flicker, but presently, as my eyes grew accustomed to the light, details of the room within emerged slowly from the mist, strange animals, statues and gold – everywhere the glint of gold.'

It was the first light to fall on the room for over 3,200 years. Carter remained silent as he watched the candle dance over glimmers of gold in the dark interior with its wonderful collection of extraordinary and beautiful objects heaped upon one another.

Lord Carnarvon, his sponsor, asked anxiously: 'Can you see anything?'

'Yes,' Carter replied. 'Wonderful things.'

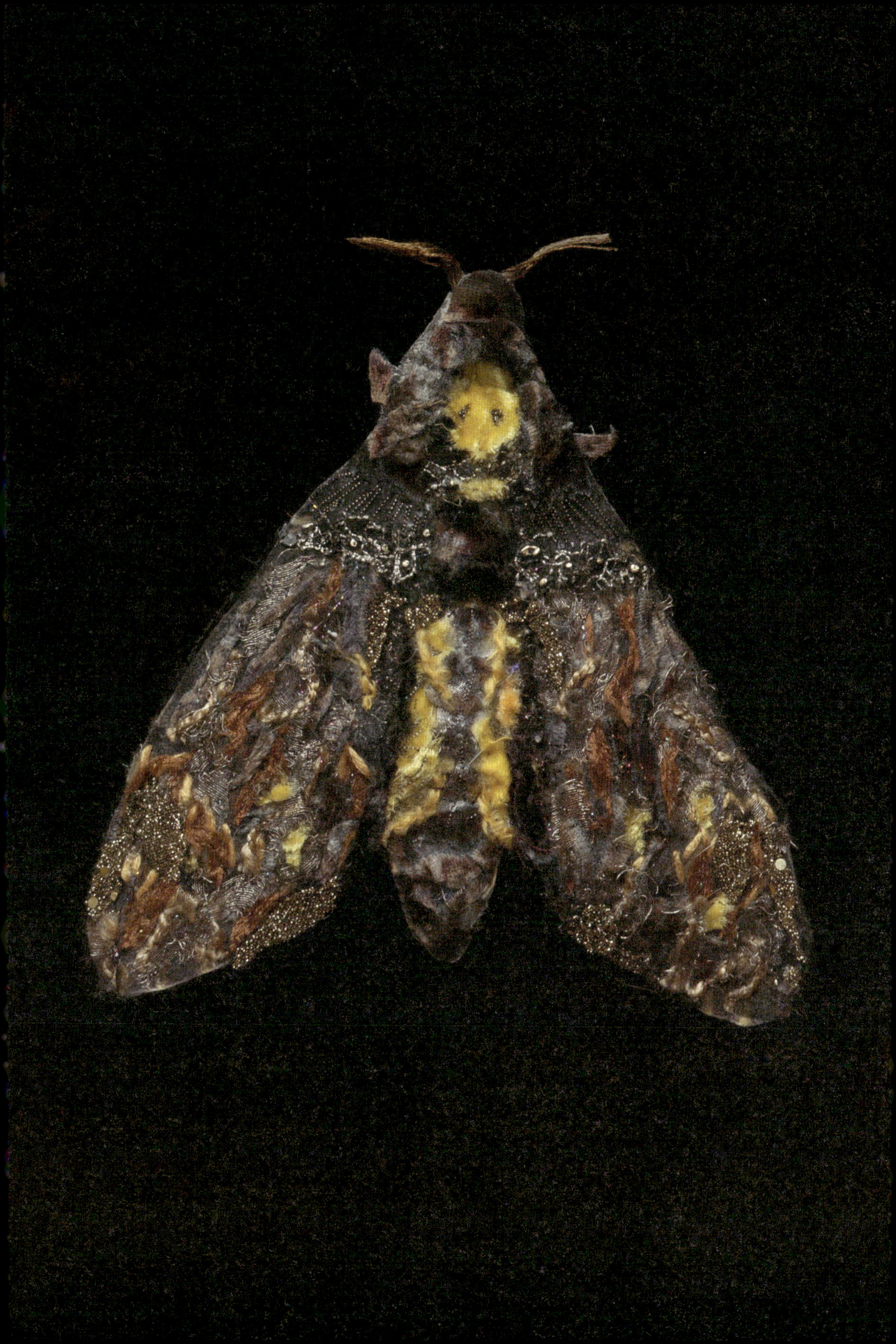

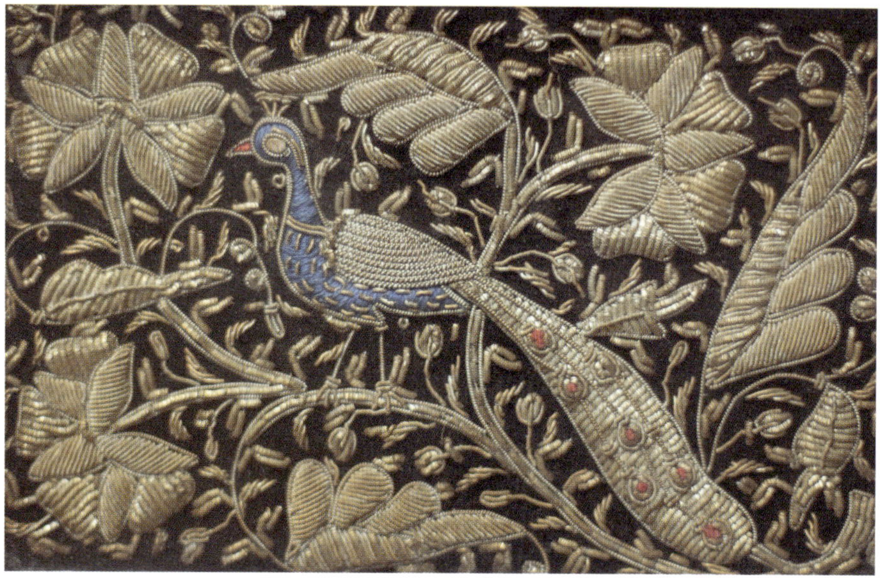

Hand embroidery is not just beautiful in itself but it is also a bewitching journey of the centuries, each piece holding within it the essence and heart of that time and having the ability to hold within it the feelings and emotions placed by the imprint of the hand that made it, so that we, too, can share them. Because it is such a tactile and mindful art form, it seems able to retain intention in a very ancient form of medicine work, placing that intention into storytelling and recording the moment with needle and thread.

These two embroideries, from different periods in the distinct cultures of India and China, illustrate this point in their interpretations of a peacock and the differing perspectives of nature they reveal.

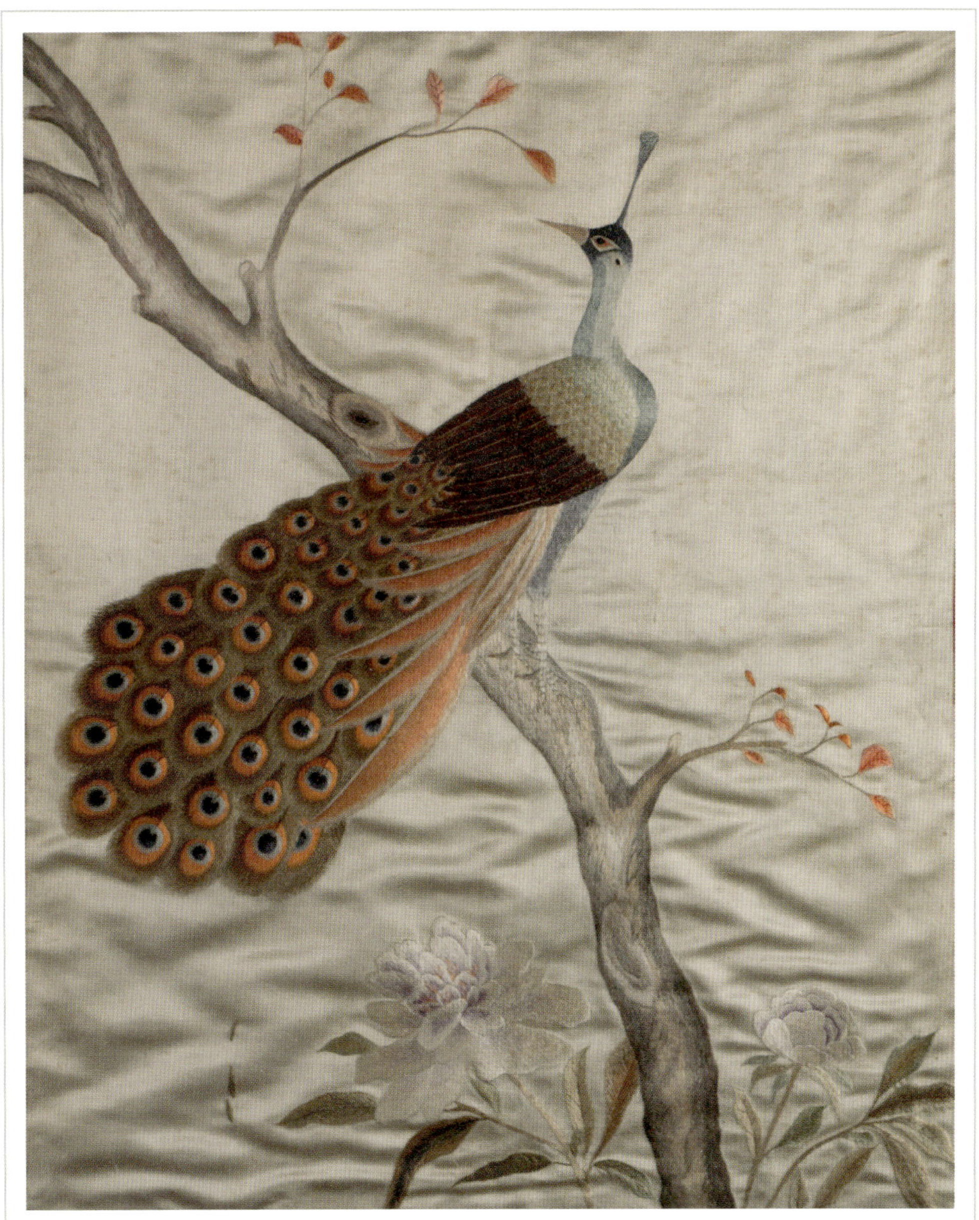

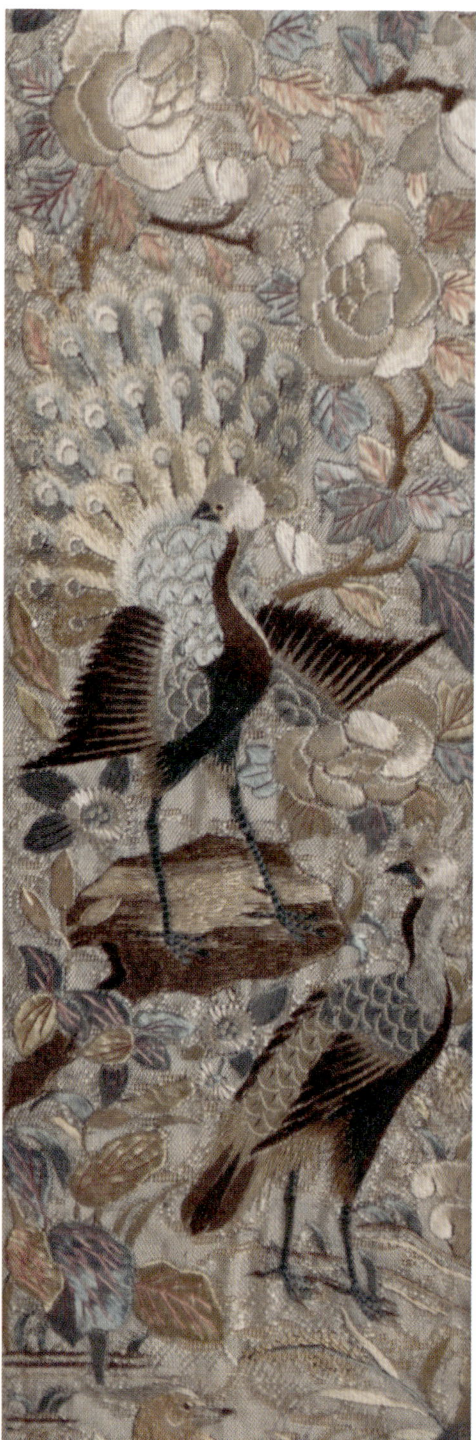

The embroideries which I love the most are the embroideries that I grew up with: Chinese embroideries. Chinese embroideries often have nature at their heart and depict the beauty of flowers, birds and insects in exquisite detail. In China, the land of silk, where silkworms have been domesticated for over 5,000 years, there is a long-standing tradition of silk embroidery. In the Forbidden City, where the emperors of China lived from the 1400s until the 1900s, especially skilled embroiderers were employed to serve the royal court.

The 'forbidden stitch', detailing rich robes, hangings and tapestries was reserved solely for the emperor and his court to enjoy. None of these embroideries was allowed to leave the Forbidden City.

This stitch was reputed to have been called the forbidden stitch, not only because it was set apart for use within the Forbidden City, but also because the stitch was so intricate that it could cause the embroiderers to go blind in the emperor's service. The stitches used silken threads that were sometimes as fine as a strand of hair.

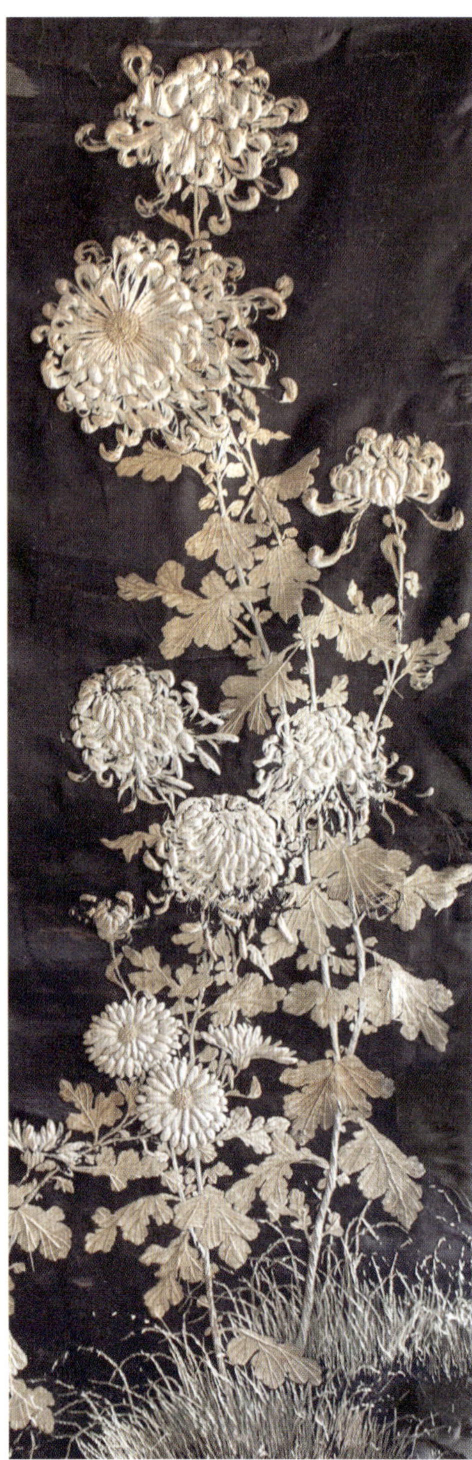

This love of honouring and depicting nature through exquisite embroidery was also found in Japan. Amazingly, I discovered these wonderful embroideries thrown away in a skip.

The art of Japanese embroidery (*nihon shishu*, literally meaning Japanese painting) dates back more than 1,600 years. The embroideries I have rely solely on complexity of stitch rather than colour to achieve richness and beauty in their portrayal of flowers.

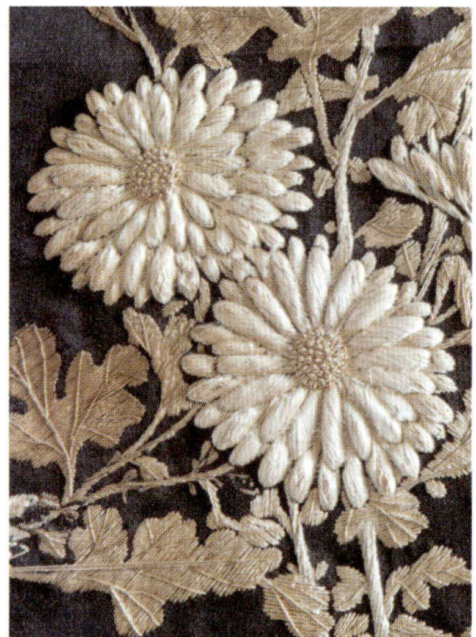

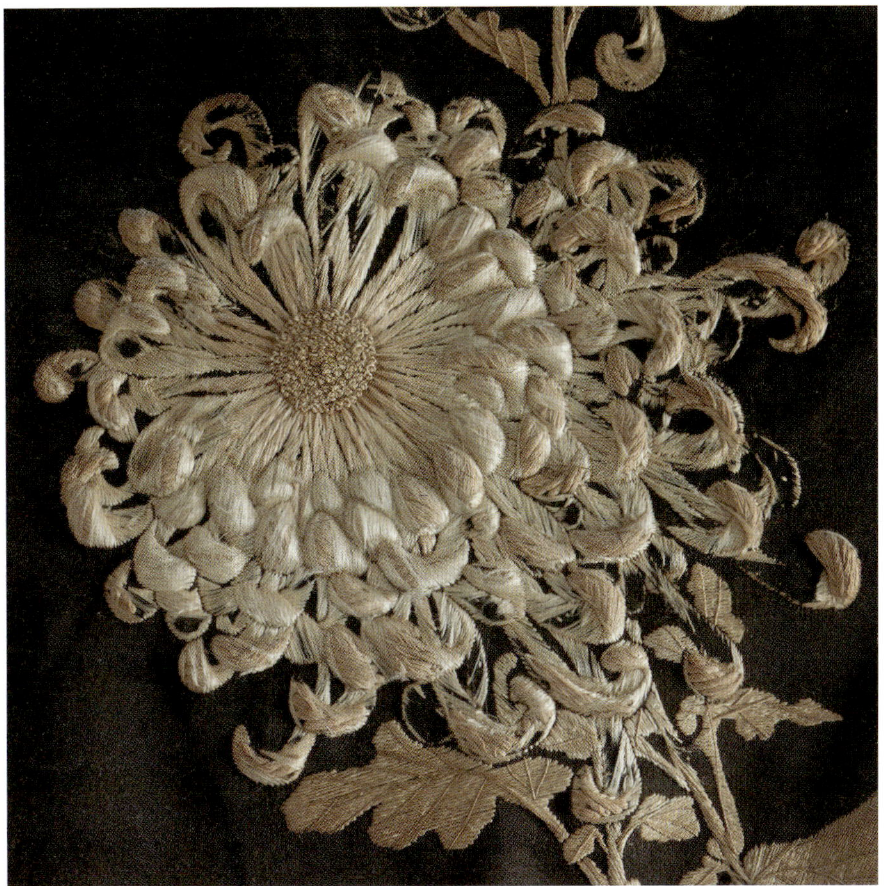

Flower motifs are one of the most common themes in Japanese embroidery. Botanical symbolism is so important in Japan that it is considered to be a language of its own (*Hanakotoba*).

Each embroidered flower can therefore be used to convey a specific emotion or sentiment without the need for the spoken word. Amongst the many flowers that are named, these are just a few examples.

Cherry blossoms symbolise the transience of life and also its renewal. Peonies are a symbol of bravery, honour and good fortune. Pine trees, because they are evergreen, represent good fortune and steadfastness. Carnations represent love and fascination, and the all-important flower, the chrysanthemum, the symbol of the emperor and the imperial family, is said to represent longevity, rejuvenation and regal beauty.

The Elizabethan and Stuart periods were regarded as the golden ages of hand embroidery. Their embroiderers were considered on a par with sculptors, painters and architects. Botanists and naturalists were also greatly valued due to their discoveries of new and exotic species in this era of navigation and exploration.

With the increase in wealth in the prosperous reign of Elizabeth I, there was money to spend. Interest in flower gardening grew, and botanical themes in embroidery came to the fore, especially as society prided itself on the cultivation of flowers and plants from the newly discovered parts of the world.

John Gerard, in the introduction to his *Herball* of 1597, likened a garden to embroidery: 'If delight may provoke men's labour, what greater delights is there then to behold the earth as apparelled with plants, as with a robe of imbroidered worke, set with orient pearles, and garnished with great diversitie of rare and costly jewels? The delight is great but the use greater, and joyned often with necessitie.' Because of the increased interest, more botanical books were then produced, which in turn gave greater inspiration for the embroiderers.

At that time, English men and women were famed throughout Europe for the richness of their clothing and furnishings. The richer the embroidery, the more it proclaimed the owner's importance. Looking at this beautifully preserved man's nightcap with its botanical theme of Tudor roses, it seems as if you can still feel the presence of the person who wore it.

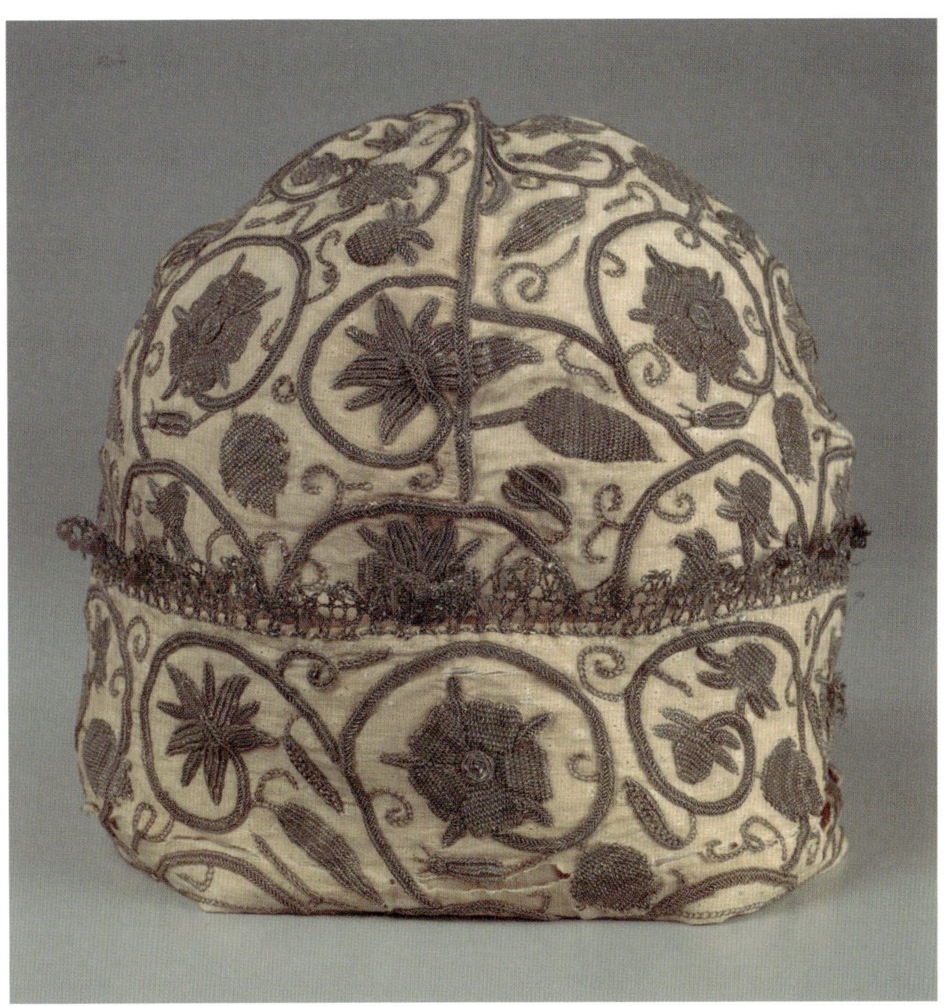

Man's nightcap, late 1500s

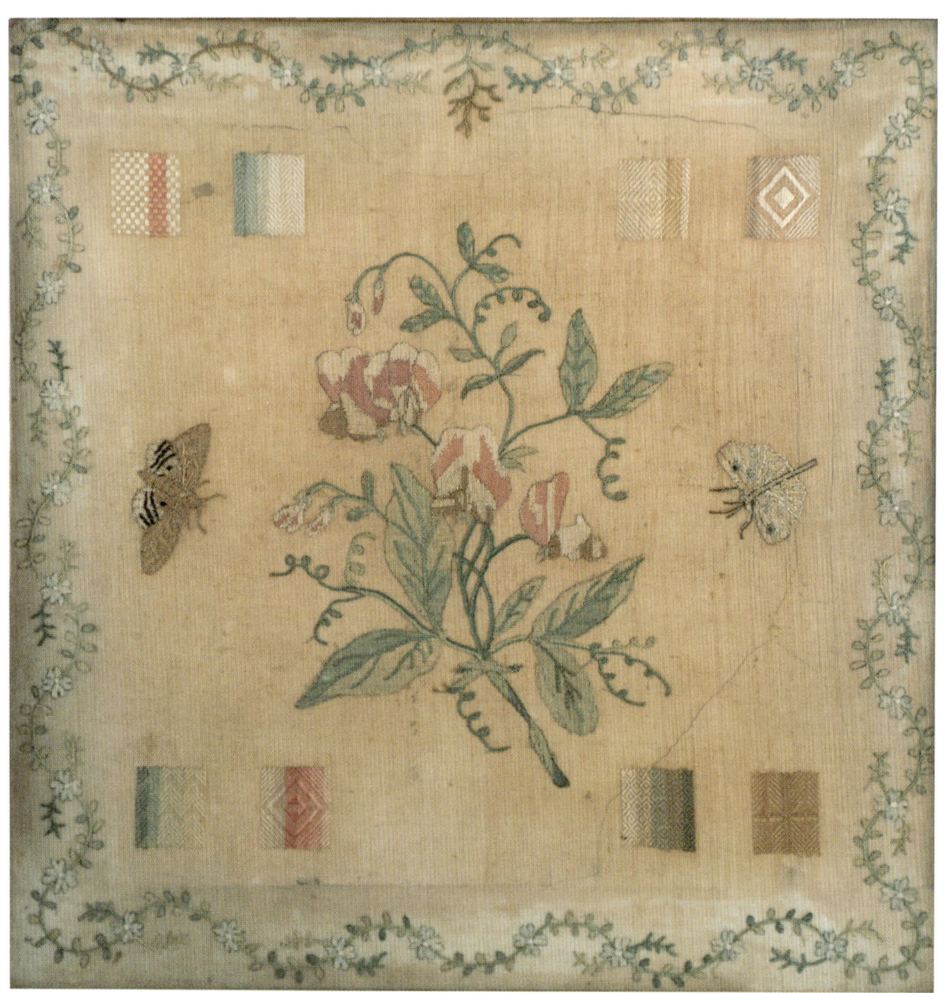

Sampler embroidered by Eliza Jones, 1794

In the eighteenth and nineteenth centuries, it had become a necessary skill for 'nicely brought up young ladies' to embroider small pieces of art, nature designs in all their variety being the favourite theme. It was also an important source of income for the less well off. Experienced embroiderers began to embroider on to small pieces of material the stitches that would produce the most beautiful, life-like images of the natural world. This being especially relevant in Victorian times when the language of flowers was considered of importance. Samplers were also simplified and used for educational purposes such as teaching the alphabet and the Bible.

Young girls would practise their stitches using these samplers and, in trying to gain employment, would then use their own samplers to showcase their work, in the same way that, nowadays, an artist uses their portfolio.

Although I have a collection of samplers, the invoked vision of young embroiderers sitting dutifully at their stitching adding to their naive charm, I also have one which contains the most minute stitching, conjuring up thoughts of the forbidden stitch in comparison.

However, this sampler is to illustrate the mundane task of darning, although the wish to include the wonder of nature still prevailed. The embroidery is beautiful, and I love the simplicity of the sweet pea at its centre. It is as if the creator is quite unaware of the beauty of the piece on its own but is simply using it to illustrate the importance of being able to darn correctly.

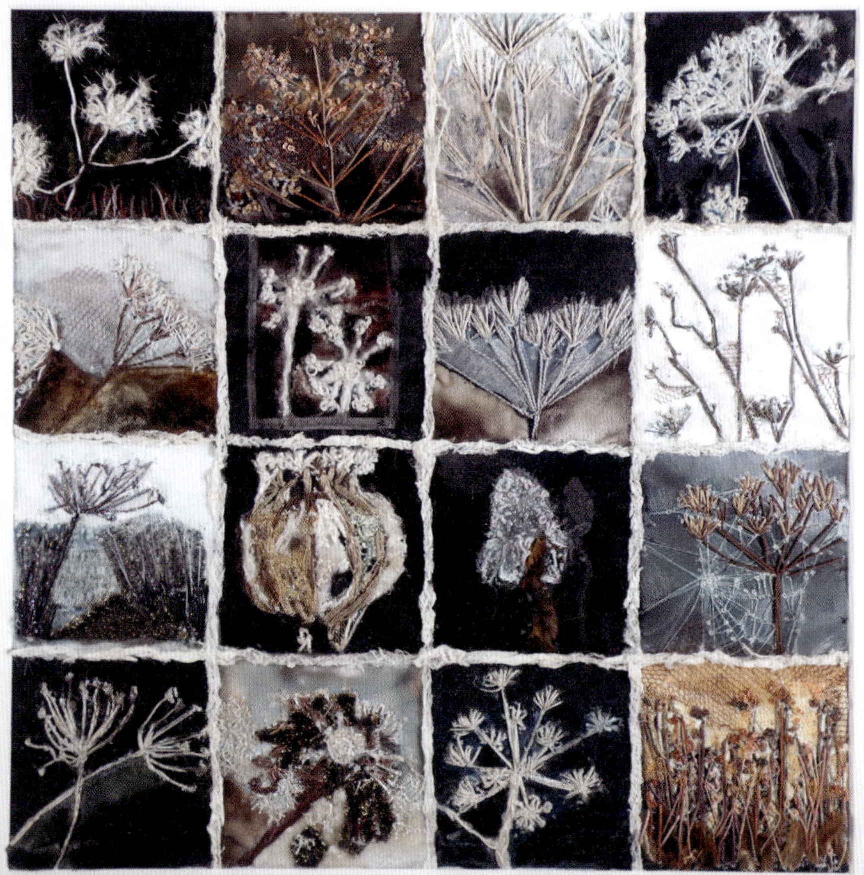

The art of trying out ideas and thoughts and design is illustrated in this embroidery – the modern-day equivalent of a sampler. I created this to experiment with different 'winter' ideas, to see the effect of ice and frost on diverse structures, with the winter season embroideries in mind.

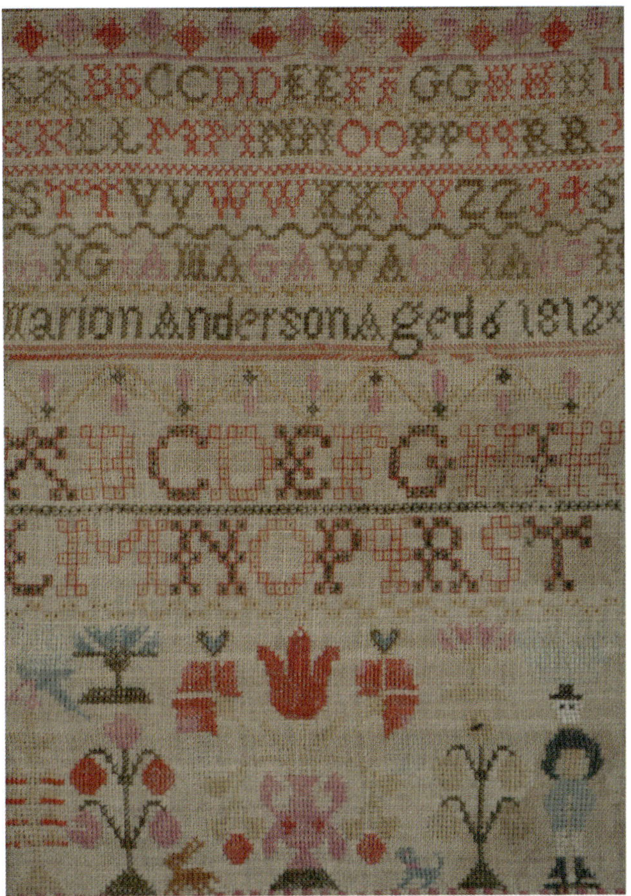

The Industrial Revolution changed the focus of working life towards industry and machine manufacturing. It was the beginning of the journey into mass production.

An embroidery machine was made in France in the mid-1800s, at which point hand embroidery became a craft rather than an art. Machine-created patterns were made to simplify the embroidery process so that it no longer required master workmanship but could be worked by anyone who wished to do so. People's minds had turned to technology rather than nature, but even so nature patterns were still the most popular and the patterns themselves could be followed with ease to produce a beautiful end result. Nature's bounty could be enjoyed and shared through a restful, creative hobby, offering respite from iron and steel and machines in remembering an arcadian existence.

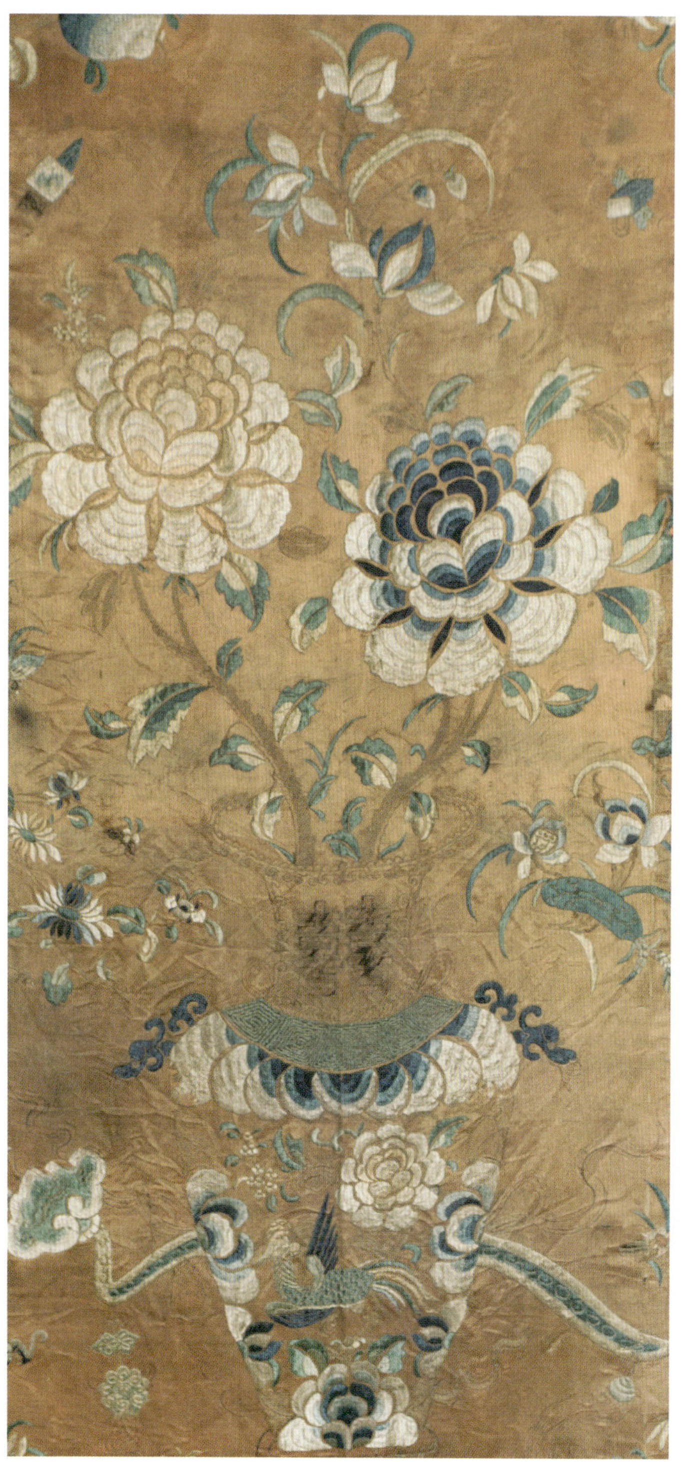

Nowadays, however, embroidery artists are once again recognised in their own right as fine art artists creating magical images of nature for the world to see. The Royal School of Needlework (the International Centre of Excellence for the Art of Hand Embroidery since 1872) celebrates this on its website, and the Worshipful Company of Broderers and the Society for Embroidered Work are well-respected advocates.

The Broderer's website states 'Great embroideries are great works of art'. Their recent exhibition emphasised this fact, incuding many stunning embroideries of the natural world, touching the soul and the senses with their beauty. The embroideries demonstrated different forms and techniques, carrying on traditions from many parts of the world.

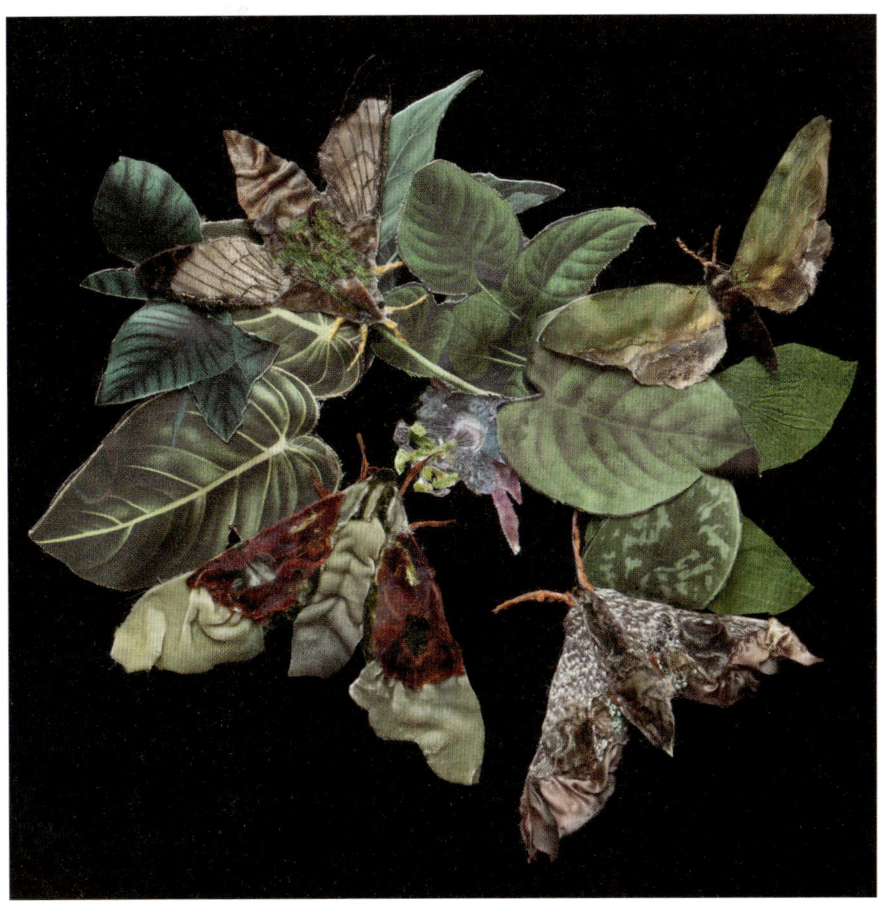

The art of hand embroidery brings colours of flowers and shapes of leaves and trees, bleached grass and golden cornfields, spiders' webs on frozen seedheads, shooting stars and Northern Lights; all seen through the eye of the needle to find the magic in the world around us. Place your finger on the silken thread of the heaven's embroidered cloths to follow the path and discover the way.

HEAVEN IS UNDER OUR FEET
AS WELL AS OVER OUR HEADS

Henry David Thoreau

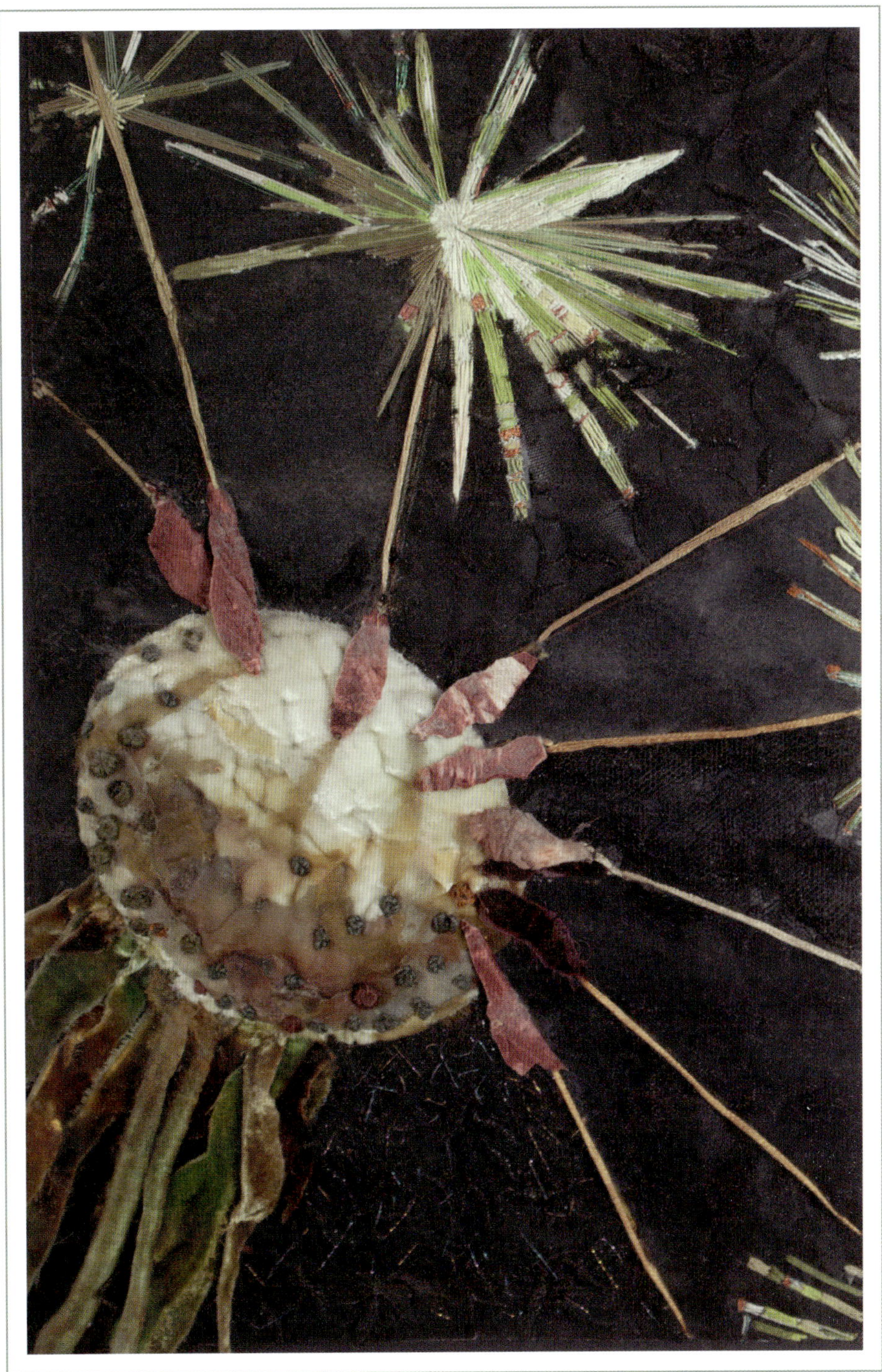

INSPIRATION

A SINCERE ARTIST IS NOT ONE WHO MAKES A FAITHFUL ATTEMPT TO PUT ONTO CANVAS WHAT IS IN FRONT OF HIM, BUT ONE WHO TRIES TO CREATE SOMETHING WHICH IS, IN ITSELF, A LIVING THING.

Sir William Dobell

IT IS NOT ONLY the life and beauty that I find in my garden and in the countryside around me that I wish to share but also the drama and theatre inherent in nature. Accidental stunning colour combinations, unexpected architectural structures, unusually intricate patterns and textures. Hand embroidery gladly lends its hand to recreate all these discoveries. An unused piece of deep-red velvet will become the perfect foil to a burnt-orange oriental poppy petal, or a tattered old piece of gold brocade will transform itself into a sycamore seed. Silk threads allow you to paint with them.

I have a magpie's treasure trove of velvets, silks and threads, crystals, shells and stained glass, Venetian masks and Zuni fetishes, fossils and dried leaves – anything, in fact, that appealed to me when I found it, all waiting in my studio to inspire me. It is an Aladdin's cave, an enticement in itself.

The starting point for me is to see something in nature that captures my imagination and to record it. I have the images from my photography as a visual reference, even though I know the work will usually take on a life of its own. The studio is overflowing, but I know where even the smallest thread is that I think would work beautifully to achieve my desired effect. I wish to make the work three-dimensional and alive and to show its heart, whether it is a butterfly, a flower or the leaf from an oak tree.

When I prepare to work, I have the image in my mind and I choose my colour palette. I choose threads and materials of different textures and the shades of colour that are suitable for the chosen subject, making sure that I have a large enough selection around me to really engage my imagination and senses. I also use watercolours and botanical art techniques to depict finer details. Then the work takes over, and I work intuitively, because the work itself shows me what texture or colour is needed next in order to grow and perhaps reveal a new aspect of itself as I embroider, and it will also tell me when it has come alive and is complete. I often 'build' the work, making it piece by piece. I sculpt with the materials and paint with the threads.

In addition to the botanical art techniques which allow me to 'paint' with silk thread, I also use structural materials and appliqué, which allows the artwork to become three-dimensional and multi-layered with rich texture and thread. I use only hand embroidery because it allows time to enter into a real understanding of the subject and to conjure. Alchemy and empathy, with nature the wellspring.

Hand embroidery contains messages within it, messages placed by the hand with intent. My desire is to share not just the beauty but also the physiological benefits – the peace, healing and wonder – that nature in all its forms freely offers us.

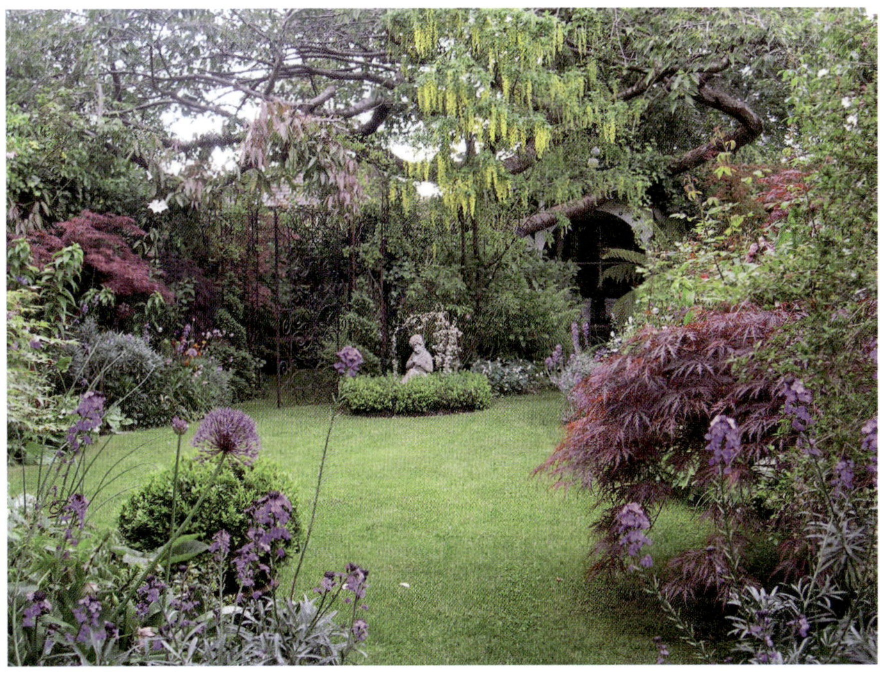

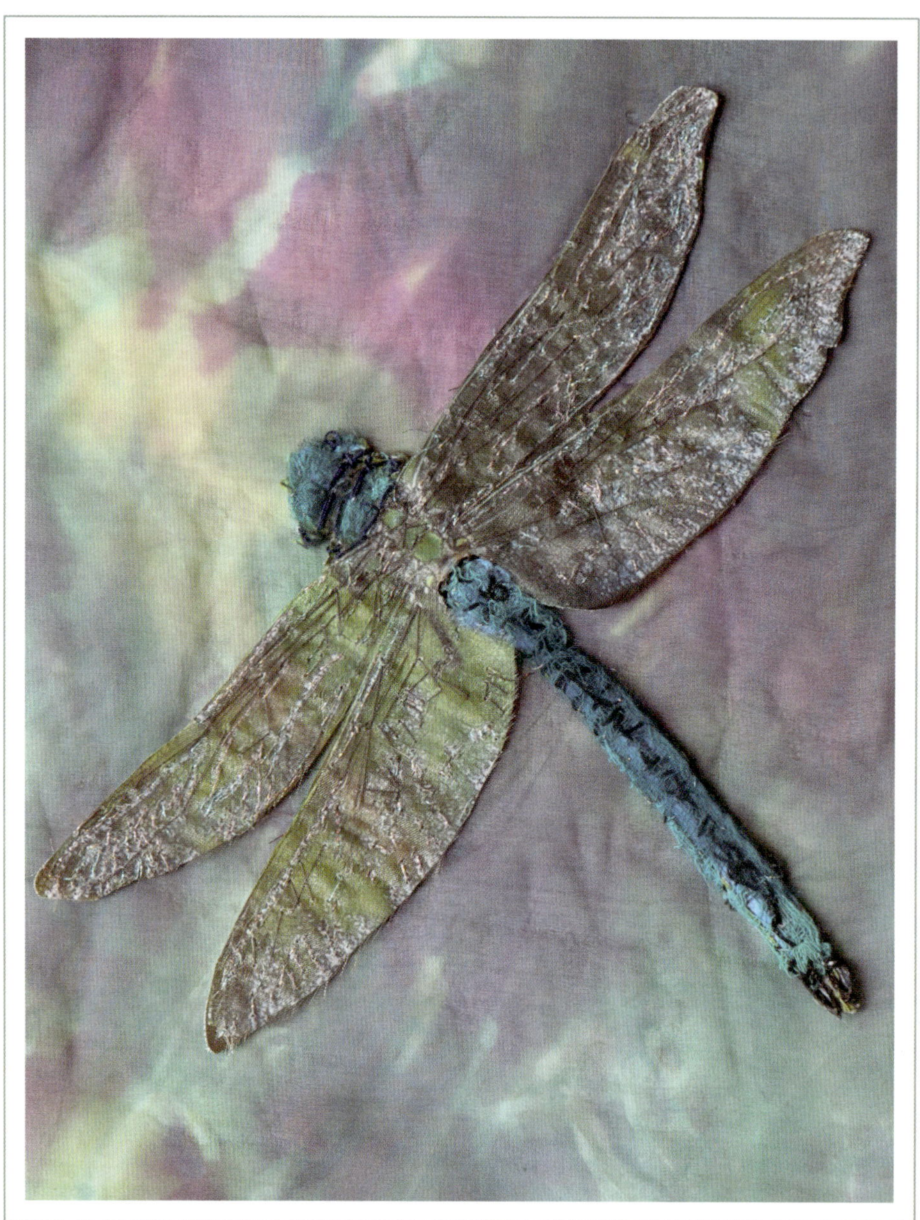

INDEX OF ILLUSTRATIONS

I would like to thank everyone involved in the making of this book, especially the following people:
David King
Ronny de Koning
Ian Strathcarron
Alex Saberi
Andy Small
Zac Goldsmith
Piers Morgan
Merlin Ambrosius
Shenoah Taylor and the Seidr group
Andrew Wayfinder
Phillip Hall
Lawrence Heyworth of Look and Learn
Lauren Glucina of Ascension Kitchen
To my friends for their advice and support.

PICTURE CREDITS
Page 102 Royal Collection Trust / © His Majesty King Charles III 2023
Pages 104, 105 Metropolitan Museum of Art, Gift of Theodore M. Davis, 1909
Page 115 Heritage Image Partnership Ltd / Alamy Stock Photo
All other images – author's collection.

Published in 2024 by Unicorn, an imprint of Unicorn Publishing Group
Charleston Studio, Meadow Business Centre Lewes BN8 5RW

www.unicornpublishing.org

ISBN 978-1-916846-04-3
10 9 8 7 6 5 4 3 2 1

Printed by Fine Tone Ltd

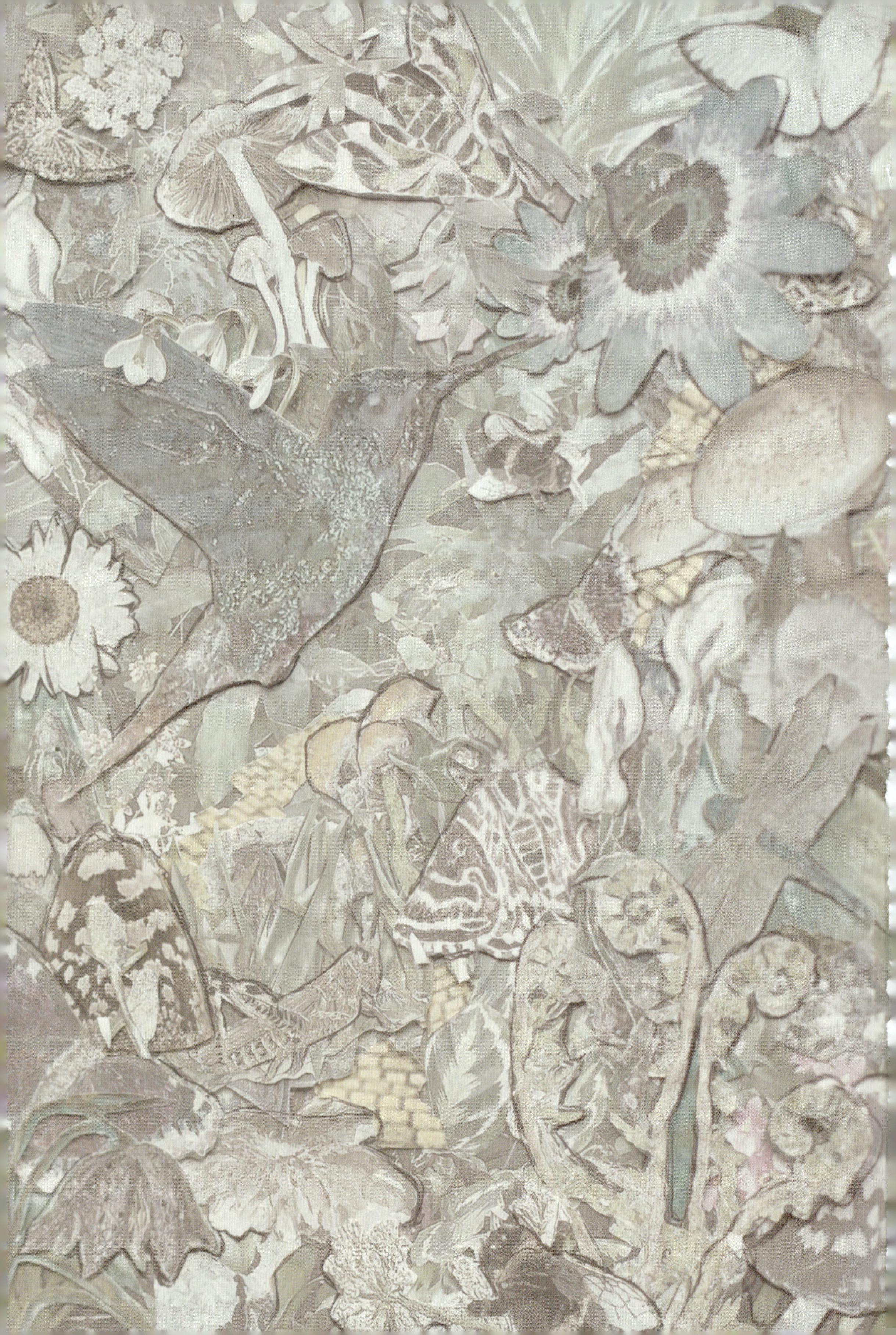